Pulpit Outlines Series
www.pulpitoutlines.com

52 Funeral Sermons

By Barry L. Davis, D.Min.

Dear Fellow Preacher,

For most of us, one of the most rewarding, yet difficult tasks, is preparing messages to preach and teach. We are honored by God to stand before our congregation each week, and we want to give them the very best, but with the press of the many demands of ministry, sometimes that is difficult to do.

And if you're like me, you prefer writing your own sermons because you have a special connection with your congregation that is hard to reach through a message someone else has written. In other words, no one knows your people like you do!

Our new Pulpit Outline Series gives you a starting point – a sermon title, a deductive sermon outline; and a relevant illustration you can use however you like.

But you are free to "fill-in-the-blanks" so to speak, and add your own meat and potatoes to the mix! We invite you to make these messages your own, because only you know the people God has called you to preach to.

And we are so honored that you've invested in our third volume in the Pulpit Outline series – 52 Funeral Sermons – there will be more to come!

NOTE: In this Special Edition you will find that we have not included an opening illustration, as that time will normally be filled with a eulogy, or other words about the deceased.

May God Bless You as You Share His Word!

In Christ,

Barry L. Davis

Barry L. Davis, D.Min.

www.pastorshelper.com | www.pulpitoutlines.com

TABLE OF CONTENTS

1. THE LIFE BEYOND

And I heard a voice from heaven saying unto me, Write, Blessed are the dead which die in the Lord from henceforth: Yea, saith the Spirit, that they may rest from their labours; and their works do follow them. – Revelation 14:13

The Bible teaches that life does not end at the grave. The eternal spirit and image of God within us cannot be destroyed by the death of the body. John must have had this truth in mind when he wrote Revelation 14:13.

Obviously, this is a view of death from the other side. Viewed from our vantage point, death appears to be dreadful, defeating, and devastating. But from God's vantage point, it is altogether different. He calls the dead, "blessed." That word literally means "happy," "to be congratulated," "fortunate." Far from being pitied, God tells us that those who die with faith in the Lord are to be envied.

1. THE DOORWAY TO REST

> *1) Death is the doorway to rest from our labors.* The word "labor" describes a wearing out from work, a wearisome toil. It suggests to us that life is often hard. It can be full of difficulties, disappointments, and disease. God promises us rest from all of that.

> *2) Death is the doorway into that rest for God's people.* We need to thank God for death. There comes a time when we need to lay down our burden and to be at rest. The word "rest" that appears here is

a beautiful word. It means to be at ease, to be refreshed. It suggests an end to the toils and tribulations of life.

This is what Jesus promised to us when He said:

Come unto me, all ye that labour and are heavy laden, and I will give you rest. Take my yoke upon you, and learn of me; for I am meek and lowly in heart: and ye shall find rest unto your souls. For my yoke is easy, and my burden is light. – Matthew 11:28-30

In this world of trouble, we can know rest. But there is a greater and more complete rest for us when we go to be with the Lord. It is the rest of heaven and the presence of God. And those who have laid their burden down and entered into it are to be congratulated – they are truly fortunate.

2. DOORWAY TO REWARD

Johns says in Revelation 14, "their works do follow them." We are all making a record on earth. We carry the record of our life with us into eternity. By the lives that we live, by the words that we say, and the deeds that we do, we are laying up for ourselves treasures in heaven. Jesus said if we give a cup of cold water to a little child because we are His disciple, we will in no way lose our reward (Matt. 10:42). The Bible tells us that God will not forget our works and labor of love which we have done in His name as we minister to others (Heb. 6:10). Our works follow us. They accompany us to the very judgment of God.

The purpose of the judgment is not to determine our destiny but to determine our reward in that destiny. We are saved by grace, but we will be rewarded by our works. If we have lived faithfully and served our Lord lovingly then death becomes the doorway to our reward. And those who have gone to a good reward are fortunate. They are to be congratulated.

3. DOORWAY TO RESURRECTION

While the resurrection is not mentioned in this verse, it is affirmed in 1 Corinthians 15:20-22:

But now is Christ risen from the dead, and become the firstfruits of them that slept. For since by man came death, by man came also the resurrection of the dead. For as in Adam all die, even so in Christ shall all be made alive. – 1 Corinthians 15:20-22

The Bible teaches more than the immortality or the survival of the spirit of man. It also teaches the resurrection of the body. Those who die in Christ go immediately to be with the Lord. And when Christ returns the body that has died will come to life again. It will be a new and glorious resurrection body and will be like the resurrected body of Christ. As His body was recognizable, so our friend and loved one will be recognizable also. As His body transcended the limitations of time and space, so our body will not be subject to the limitations of this life. As His body was no longer subject to disease and decay, so our body will be an immortal body.
It will live forever.

2. THE CHRISTIAN'S HOME

For we know that if our earthly house of this tabernacle were dissolved, we have a building of God, an house not made with hands, eternal in the heavens. For in this we groan, earnestly desiring to be clothed upon with our house which is from heaven: If so be that being clothed we shall not be found naked. For we that are in this tabernacle do groan, being burdened: not for that we would be unclothed, but clothed upon, that mortality might be swallowed up of life. Now he that hath wrought us for the selfsame thing is God, who also hath given unto us the earnest of the Spirit. Therefore we are always confident, knowing that, whilst we are at home in the body, we are absent from the Lord: (For we walk by faith, not by sight:) We are confident, I say, and willing rather to be absent from the body, and to be present with the Lord. – 2 Corinthians 5:1-8

We are gathered here today to pay tribute to our dear sister in Christ. We know that for all of us this is a time of sorrow--but it is a time of sorrow mixed with joy. It's a time of sorrow because:

We realize that for a time we will not be able to see our loved one. Sorrow because of a touch that will not be felt. Sorrow because of a smile that will not be seen. Sorrow because of a laugh that will not be heard. Sorrow because of a voice that no longer beckons us near. Sorrow because of a love that will be remembered, but not experienced firsthand. Yes, there is sorrow in this time of death – but there is also great joy.

There is great joy today because: the woman we honor is a Christian. Joy because she had turned her life over to the Lord. Joy because she had been bathed in the blood of the

Lamb. Joy because she made the decision to embrace the cross of Calvary. Joy because through the power of the resurrection she now dwells in an eternal home promised to her by Jesus Christ our Lord.

And we have joy in knowing that our dear sister in Christ now spends her days where every tear is wiped away; where there is no longer any death, or mourning or crying or pain. We can have joy in knowing that she is home.

1. HER DEAREST ONES ARE THERE

Many of her dear one's are still here with us. But although those whom she has loved on earth aren't with her now, that doesn't mean that she's alone.

1) God is there. He has called her home and was waiting for her with open arms. Can you imagine the joy of finally being in the presence of the One who created the universe? The joy of hearing the voice of the One who commanded the light to be separated from the darkness saying, "Welcome Home"? The joy of experiencing the presence of One who is all-powerful; all-knowing; and in all-places at all times? The joy of being with the One who calls Himself "I Am"?

2) Jesus is there. He bid her welcome into His eternal Kingdom. Oh, what joy to see the One who shed His blood on Calvary so that all who have surrendered their lives to Him could enter into this place of perfection. To touch the hands and feet that were pierced for the sins of the world. To be so close to the One who gave His life, so that we could have eternal life.

3) The Saints are there. All of the Christians who left this earth before her are there with her now. Christian friends who she has grieved over because she no longer had their fellowship – they are there. That fellowship has been renewed now. The Saints who have gone before are there and can welcome her home.

2. SHE BELONGS THERE

The Bible teaches us that this present world is not the real home of the Christian. Peter begins his first letter by addressing the Christians as "strangers" in this world. Again in 1 Peter 2:11 he addresses the believers in the same way – as "aliens and pilgrims" in the world.

Christians who live on this earth do not really belong here. We are here for a temporary purpose--to glorify God--but our true home is in Heaven.

The good news is that our loved one no longer lives as an "alien and stranger" in this world. She is at home with the Lord where she belongs. She is where she was meant to be. She is where God created her to be. She is at a place that can truly be called "home." She is absent from her body and at home with the Lord.

Let not your heart be troubled: ye believe in God, believe also in me. In my Father's house are many mansions: if it were not so, I would have told you. I go to prepare a place for you. And if I go and prepare a place for you, I will come again, and receive you unto myself; that where I am, there ye may be also. – John 14:1-3

3. BUT A STEP, THEN DEATH

And David sware moreover, and said, Thy father certainly knoweth that I have found grace in thine eyes; and he saith, Let not Jonathan know this, lest he be grieved: but truly as the LORD liveth, and as thy soul liveth, there is but a step between me and death. – 1 Samuel 20:3

1. DEATH IS A STEP WE ALL MUST TAKE

For that which befalleth the sons of men befalleth beasts; even one thing befalleth them: as the one dieth, so dieth the other; yea, they have all one breath; so that a man hath no preeminence above a beast: for all is vanity. All go unto one place; all are of the dust, and all turn to dust again. – Ecclesiastes 3:19-20

There is no man that hath power over the spirit to retain the spirit; neither hath he power in the day of death: and there is no discharge in that war; neither shall wickedness deliver those that are given to it. – Ecclesiastes 8:8

2. DEATH IS STEP OF UNKNOWN TIMING

For man also knoweth not his time: as the fishes that are taken in an evil net, and as the birds that are caught in the snare; so are the sons of men snared in an evil time, when it falleth suddenly upon them. – Ecclesiastes 9:12

Go to now, ye that say, To day or to morrow we will go into such a city, and continue there a year, and buy and sell, and get gain: Whereas ye know not what shall be on the morrow. For what is your life? It is even a vapour, that

appeareth for a little time, and then vanisheth away. –
James 4:13-14

But God said unto him, Thou fool, this night thy soul shall be required of thee: then whose shall those things be, which thou hast provided? – Luke 12:20

3. DEATH IS A PARTING STEP

As the cloud is consumed and vanisheth away: so he that goeth down to the grave shall come up no more. He shall return no more to his house, neither shall his place know him any more. – Job 7:9-10

Therefore we are always confident, knowing that, whilst we are at home in the body, we are absent from the Lord: -
2 Corinthians 5:6

4. DEATH IS A STEP THAT MUST BE TAKEN ALONE, OR WITH CHRIST

Yea, though I walk through the valley of the shadow of death, I will fear no evil: for thou art with me; thy rod and thy staff they comfort me. – Psalm 23:4

When thou passest through the waters, I will be with thee; and through the rivers, they shall not overflow thee: when thou walkest through the fire, thou shalt not be burned; neither shall the flame kindle upon thee. – Isaiah 43:2

But he, being full of the Holy Ghost, looked up stedfastly into heaven, and saw the glory of God, and Jesus standing on the right hand of God... And they stoned Stephen, calling upon God, and saying, Lord Jesus, receive my spirit. – Acts 7:55, 59

5. PREPARATION FOR THIS STEP IS NECESSARY

For the wages of sin is death; but the gift of God is eternal life through Jesus Christ our Lord. – Romans 6:23

The sting of death is sin; and the strength of sin is the law. – 1 Corinthians 15:56

In the fear of the LORD is strong confidence: and his children shall have a place of refuge. The fear of the LORD is a fountain of life, to depart from the snares of death. – Proverbs 14:26-27

But Christ as a son over his own house; whose house are we, if we hold fast the confidence and the rejoicing of the hope firm unto the end. – Hebrews 3:6

4. BLESSED ARE THE DEAD

And I heard a voice from heaven saying unto me, Write, Blessed are the dead which die in the Lord from henceforth: Yea, saith the Spirit, that they may rest from their labours; and their works do follow them. – Revelation 14:13

1. DECAY AND DEATH ARE WRITTEN EVERYWHERE

And as it is appointed unto men once to die, but after this the judgment. – Hebrews 9:27

For that which befalleth the sons of men befalleth beasts; even one thing befalleth them: as the one dieth, so dieth the other; yea, they have all one breath; so that a man hath no preeminence above a beast: for all is vanity. – Ecclesiastes 3:19

2. DECAY AND DEATH ARE CONQUERED BY JESUS

I am he that liveth, and was dead; and, behold, I am alive for evermore, Amen; and have the keys of hell and of death. – Revelation 1:18

Forasmuch then as the children are partakers of flesh and blood, he also himself likewise took part of the same; that through death he might destroy him that had the power of death, that is, the devil; And deliver them who through fear of death were all their lifetime subject to bondage. – Hebrews 2:14-15

3. THE DEAD ARE BLESSED IN THE LORD

And the ransomed of the LORD shall return, and come to Zion with songs and everlasting joy upon their heads: they shall obtain joy and gladness, and sorrow and sighing shall flee away. – Isaiah 35:10

But I would not have you to be ignorant, brethren, concerning them which are asleep, that ye sorrow not, even as others which have no hope. For if we believe that Jesus died and rose again, even so them also which sleep in Jesus will God bring with him. – 1 Thessalonians 4:13-14

Let not your heart be troubled: ye believe in God, believe also in me. In my Father's house are many mansions: if it were not so, I would have told you. I go to prepare a place for you. And if I go and prepare a place for you, I will come again, and receive you unto myself; that where I am, there ye may be also. – John 14:1-3

4. THE DEAD ARE HAPPY WITH THE LORD

To an inheritance incorruptible, and undefiled, and that fadeth not away, reserved in heaven for you, Who are kept by the power of God through faith unto salvation ready to be revealed in the last time. – 1 Peter 1:4-5

5. RIPE FOR HARVESTING

Thou shalt come to thy grave in a full age, like as a shock of corn cometh in in his season. – Job 5:26

1. THE SEED SOWN – LIFE'S OPPORTUNITY

He that observeth the wind shall not sow; and he that regardeth the clouds shall not reap. As thou knowest not what is the way of the spirit, nor how the bones do grow in the womb of her that is with child: even so thou knowest not the works of God who maketh all. In the morning sow thy seed, and in the evening withhold not thine hand: for thou knowest not whether shall prosper, either this or that, or whether they both shall be alike good. – Ecclesiastes 11:4-6

Be not deceived; God is not mocked: for whatsoever a man soweth, that shall he also reap. For he that soweth to his flesh shall of the flesh reap corruption; but he that soweth to the Spirit shall of the Spirit reap life everlasting. – Galatians 6:7-8

Sow to yourselves in righteousness, reap in mercy; break up your fallow ground: for it is time to seek the LORD, till he come and rain righteousness upon you. – Hosea 10:12

Being born again, not of corruptible seed, but of incorruptible, by the word of God, which liveth and abideth for ever. – 1 Peter 1:23

2. THE GROWTH – GOOD SOIL

But other fell into good ground, and brought forth fruit, some an hundredfold, some sixtyfold, some thirtyfold. – Matthew 13:8

The righteous shall flourish like the palm tree: he shall grow like a cedar in Lebanon. Those that be planted in the house of the LORD shall flourish in the courts of our God. They shall still bring forth fruit in old age; they shall be fat and flourishing. – Psalm 92:12-14

But speaking the truth in love, may grow up into him in all things, which is the head, even Christ. – Ephesians 4:15

3. THE FRUIT – A HOLY LIFE

But the fruit of the Spirit is love, joy, peace, longsuffering, gentleness, goodness, faith, Meekness, temperance: against such there is no law. – Galatians 5:22-23

A good name is better than precious ointment; and the day of death than the day of one's birth. – Ecclesiastes 7:1

4. THE HARVEST HOME – A TIME FOR JOY

Thou hast multiplied the nation, and not increased the joy: they joy before thee according to the joy in harvest, and as men rejoice when they divide the spoil. – Isaiah 9:3

But unto you that fear my name shall the Sun of righteousness arise with healing in his wings; and ye shall go forth, and grow up as calves of the stall. – Malachi 4:2

And the ransomed of the LORD shall return, and come to Zion with songs and everlasting joy upon their heads: they shall obtain joy and gladness, and sorrow and sighing shall flee away. – Isaiah 35:10

And another angel came out of the temple, crying with a loud voice to him that sat on the cloud, Thrust in thy sickle, and reap: for the time is come for thee to reap; for the harvest of the earth is ripe. – Revelation 14:15

6. THE LAST CHANGE

If a man die, shall he live again? all the days of my appointed time will I wait, till my change come. – Job 14:14

This was a very natural mode of expression for the Patriarch Job. His life was a weary monotony at the time he said these words. Day after day there was the same repressing presence of pain, reproach, and temptation. How regularly they came; how seldom they withdrew, even for an hour. What a gospel rang out of the word *"Change"* into the ear and heart of Job. Let's cheer our hearts with meditation on the certain change awaiting us all.

1. IT MAY BE AN UNWELCOME CHANGE

It is to some. The grave casts its shadow across their lives. But Jesus came to save us from the fear of death, as well as from all other fears. Death is robbed of its real sting; take heed lest, through unbelief, you invest it with an imaginary one.

So when this corruptible shall have put on incorruption, and this mortal shall have put on immortality, then shall be brought to pass the saying that is written, Death is swallowed up in victory. O death, where is thy sting? O grave, where is thy victory? – 1 Corinthians 15:54-55

2. IT WILL BE A GREAT CHANGE

Our familiar calling, the body, our relations in the world, must be left for a noble calling—a spiritual body—and for the spirits of the just. Yet, in heaven, the newest resident feels no sense of unease. Although all things are so different from those he has just left, he feels heaven is his home.

3. IT MAY BE A SUDDEN CHANGE

Sudden death, in the case of holy men and women, can be a mark of the Divine favor, as far as those taken from the world are concerned.

It is dreadful when a man is snatched away, not from honest labor and patient suffering, but from yielding to idleness, and anxiety or doubts.

4. IT IS LIKELY TO BE AN UNATTENDED CHANGE

We must die alone; the only one from your church, your city, your town. Yet, though alone in the time of death, what a wonderful company of angels shall receive you and bear you to rest.

5. IT MUST BE A FINAL CHANGE

The experience of celestial beings will know nothing of "change"; for our idea of change is connected with painful separation and uncertainty.

7. THE UNCERTAINTY OF LIFE

Take ye heed, watch and pray: for ye know not when the time is. – Mark 13:33

The veiling of the future is a mercy for most of us. We are permitted to hold undisturbed possession of all the innocent joys of life up to the time of our departure.

1. THE FACT OF LIFE'S UNCERTAINTY

Two related facts draw our attention:

1) The certainty of death.

Death is inevitable. We are born to die. Nature teaches us that our end will come.

2) The nearness of death.

We all must die soon. How soon we cannot tell.

Some are called to account in the midst of their everyday life. Their employment may be commendable, their aims good, their motives right. But, when "the time" arrives, they must leave all.

Some are taken in the very act of sin and rebellion against God. The Scriptures furnish instances of the sudden doom of those who were in rebellion: the contemporaries of Noah, the fellow-townsmen of Lot, Korah, and his companions.

But the wicked are not the only ones liable to sudden death. No degree of morality, faith, or holiness can shield any of us from it. Many good people have even desired to go suddenly. The first death was the sudden call of righteous Abel.

2. THE DUTY OF LIFE'S UNCERTAINTY

"Take heed." Many are heedless and unprepared to die. This heed-lessness arises from—The absorbing nature of earthly riches. Idleness. Ignorance. Heedlessness will cause you to miss heaven. It will land you in the place of torment. It will render you unfit for the coming of the king of terrors.

Watch and pray. Live habitually prepared for your end.

Observe these three things:

>1) Habitually believe in Christ.

>All preparation for eternity lies there. Christ is all in all.

>2) Habitually commune with God.

>Communion with God takes place with conversion. Adoption gives us connection, and opens the communication between the soul and God.

>3) Habitually aim at Christian consistency.

>We owe duty both to God and man. Christian faith must begin with God; it must extend to society.

Here is a warning to those who are neither watching nor praying.

Here is a reproof to the lukewarm professor and the backslider.

Here is encouragement to the earnest, expectant, watching believer.

8. THE CERTAINTY OF DEATH

For we must needs die, and are as water spilt on the ground, which cannot be gathered up again; neither doth God respect any person: yet doth he devise means, that his banished be not expelled from him. – 2 Samuel 14:14

1. DEATH IS CERTAIN

Death stares at us upon all sides. The fields the other day were green; now they are brown. The tree that stood by our door last year was a thing of beauty; now nothing is left but the old lifeless trunk. In our childhood there were strong men who were wonders to us because of their deeds of manly strength. Where are they now? Go read their names on the gravestones, or see them pass by the gate with decay and death written in every feature of their faces.

So God teaches in His word:

For all flesh is as grass, and all the glory of man as the flower of grass. The grass withereth, and the flower thereof falleth away. – 1 Peter 1:24

2. DEATH IS OFTEN SUDDEN

Read the columns of the newspapers, and notice how many have been recently launched into eternity.

How few really expect death when it comes!

God would teach us that life is brief; "But a hand-breadth;" "A vapor;" "A flower of the field." That its end is uncertain. Christ said that He would come "as a thief in the night." "You do not know what a day may bring forth."

3. DEATH ENDS ALL

"Water spilt on the ground which cannot be gathered up again."

Lazarus was told of a great gulf which was fixed.

The foolish virgins found the door shut for all eternity.

And as it is appointed unto men once to die, but after this the judgment. – Hebrews 9:27

4. PREPARATION FOR DEATH IS NECESSARY

All realize this as far as this world goes, but few seem to realize its importance when the next world is taken into consideration.

We fail to understand that:

The things which are seen are temporal; but the things which are not seen are eternal. – 2 Corinthians 4:18b

These "eternal" things need to be prepared for.

Because we are strong it seems to us as if we would live here forever, and we fail to heed Christ's words, "you also be ready."

How are we to make this preparation?

Jesus saith unto him, I am the way, the truth, and the life: no man cometh unto the Father, but by me. – John 14:6

Yea, though I walk through the valley of the shadow of death, I will fear no evil: for thou art with me; thy rod and thy staff they comfort me. – Psalm 23:4

O death, where is thy sting? O grave, where is thy victory? – 1 Corinthians 15:55

9. PREPARATION FOR DEATH

Be ye therefore ready also: for the Son of man cometh at an hour when ye think not. – Luke 12:40

Into Jesus' lips grace was poured. There was no subject of importance He did not explain; no duty He did not enforce; no error He did not expose; no danger he did not point out. Fully acquainted, not merely with the secrets of nature, but with the mysteries of the unseen world, He brought time and eternity, the visible and the invisible, the passing and the permanent, within the range of His teaching, and the knowledge of His disciples.

He carries you to the excellent glory, and you behold the nations of the redeemed, enjoying the kingdom prepared for them. And so it is that our Lord himself dwells upon this subject, and appeals to the consciousness of immortality that dwells within us—to the lingering spark of Divine life that still flickers unextinguished amidst the almost total ruin of our nature.

"Be ye therefore ready also." These words suggest two ideas to us today:

1. WE ARE DEPENDENT UPON AN UNSEEN CERTAINTY

Comparing death with the coming of the Son of man; both uncertain: no calculations can anticipate it; no preparations postpone it. Yet, there seems to be no limits to the attainments of human understanding in other areas. We have discovered the height of the heavens, and the distances of the stars; calculated the weight of the atmosphere in the most distant planets; and arranged invisible microscopic organisms, discoverable only by the microscope, into their genera and species. We have dived into the depths of the ocean, and brought up the treasures of the deep; into the bowels of the earth, and ransacked the center of the globe, for the wealth of our cities; we have discovered the origin of almost every disease; and traced to its source every kind of contagion. We have found out, in the animal and vegetable kingdoms, remedies to all disorders, and relief for all pain; but we have never been able to determine *when we shall die*. Few as our days are, we do not know their limit; all the days of our appointed time we must wait, whether we want to or not. The bounds of our habitation are fixed by heaven's immutable decree. Man, the creature of a day, must abide the coming of the Son of man. A tenant at will,—a little child who is to abide in a certain place till someone shall come for him, and then he must depart.

2. WE ARE DEPENDENT UPON THE SOVEREIGN CONTROL OF CHRIST

The coming of the Son of man. Who is this that comes and goes, and opens and shuts, that allows one man to continue,—but commands another away;—that has the keys of the invisible world?

He says:

I am he that liveth, and was dead; and, behold, I am alive for evermore, Amen; and have the keys of hell and of death. – Revelation 1:18

Happy are those who can say, "I know in whom I have believed." Happy are those who, as they see Him approaching, feel no crushing fear, but look on Him as one whom they have long known, and long loved, and long desired to see; so that the love of Christ casts out the fear of death; and the certainty that rest and triumph are at hand, overcome the terrors of death, and the desolation of the grave; while they are enabled, through God's grace, and the love of the Spirit, to say:

And it shall be said in that day, Lo, this is our God; we have waited for him, and he will save us: this is the LORD; we have waited for him, we will be glad and rejoice in his salvation. – Isaiah 25:9

Jesus said, *"Be ye therefore ready also."* Now, if there were nothing beyond the grave, such a command as this would be a presumptive falsehood, and a wretched mockery of the woes of man. Here is implied,

1) The immortality of the soul.

2) A conviction of the fallen condition of our nature.

3) An acceptance of the redemptive truths of Christianity.

10. DEATH AVOIDED

"And whosoever liveth and believeth in me shall <u>never die</u>. Believest thou this?" – John 11:26

Never die! What does this mean? Does it mean:

1) Freedom from physical death?

The world does not dread anything so much as death and nothing would it hail with greater joy than a deliverance from it. But so long as humankind is sinful, a deliverance from physical death would be something evil rather than something good. Death serves to arrest the course of sin, and to prevent the world from becoming chaos. Does it mean:

2) Freedom from annihilation?

We are in no danger of this; and this in itself is of no advantage:—non-existence is better than a miserable existence. What then does it mean? Generally it means this:—That nothing that gives value to life, nothing that makes life worth having, shall ever die if we truly believe in Christ.

"Verily, verily, I say unto you, He that heareth my word, and believeth on him that sent me, hath <u>everlasting life</u>, and shall not come into condemnation; but is passed from death unto life." – John 5:24

1. OUR SPIRITUAL POWERS WILL NEVER CEASE

What is life without activity? Worthless. And what is activity unless it is beneficial? Misery. Faith in Christ secures the healthy action of all our spiritual faculties. The *perceptive, reflective, imaginative, recollective, anticipative,* will work harmoniously forever.

2. OUR SPIRITUAL ACHIEVEMENTS WILL NEVER BE LOST

What is life without ideas, emotions, memories, habits? A blank. And what is it if those things are not of a truly virtuous character? Despicable and wretched. But when these acquisitions are holy, life is blessed. Faith in Christ secures the permanency and perfection of all true ideas, affections, principles, habits, etc.

And I heard a voice from heaven saying unto me, Write, Blessed are the dead which die in the Lord from henceforth: Yea, saith the Spirit, that they may rest from their labours; and their works do follow them. – Revelation 14:13

Therefore, my beloved brethren, be ye stedfast, unmoveable, always abounding in the work of the Lord, forasmuch as ye know that your labour is not in vain in the Lord. – 1 Corinthians 15:58

11. THE PALE HORSE

And I looked, and behold a pale horse: and his name that sat on him was Death, and Hell followed with him. And power was given unto them over the fourth part of the earth, to kill with sword, and with hunger, and with death, and with the beasts of the earth. – Revelation 6:8

In this chapter of the Bible we have a description of four horses with their respective riders. The first was white, on which sat an illustrious figure, with a bow, and he went forth from conquering to conquer. The second horse is red, to represent war. The third black, to represent famine: and then comes the fourth, a pale horse, whose rider is Death, and Hell followed him.

1. UNDERSTANDING THE DESCRIPTION OF DEATH

1) Death is under a seal

And when he had opened the fourth seal, I heard the voice of the fourth beast say, Come and see. – Revelation 6:7

Death is not under the direction and power of Satan, but under the author, proprietor, and disposer of Life (Deut. 33:39; Dan. 5:25; Psa. 103:4).

2) Death is represented as riding

Not as creeping, or walking, but riding forth with courage and power. Trampling as a warhorse all that come beneath his feet.

3) Death is described as a pale horse

This may denote the general appearance of mortality.

4) Death is described as being followed with Hell

This word sometimes signifies the *grave,* and death throws its victims into the cold loathsome grave. It signifies sometimes the *invisible state,* and death hurries men into the dark unknown world. It also signifies the place of *future punishment,* and death consigns the wicked to the misery of the second death.

2. UNDERSTANDING OUR DUTY CONCERNING DEATH

"I heard the voice…saying, 'Come and see.'"

1) Come and see the antiquity of death

Go and look to the world's origin, and see how soon he commenced his career.

2) Come and see the extent of devastations

No country or color, or people, ever yet escaped his ravages. Wherever man is there death is also.

3) Come and see the spoiler foiled and conquered.

Jesus in our nature entered the field of combat; for a time death prevails; but at length, Christ arises with power. His sting is withdrawn. The Savior, standing on the neck of his foe, exclaims, *"I am he that was dead," "O death, I have been thy destruction."*

4) Come and see how death may safely be encountered.

Repentance—faith in Jesus, who hath abolished death—a title for heaven, by justifying grace—a new nature—and holiness of life, without which no man can see the Lord.

12. THE ASSEMBLY OF THE SAVED

After this I beheld, and, lo, a great multitude, which no man could number, of all nations, and kindreds, and people, and tongues, stood before the throne, and before the Lamb, clothed with white robes, and palms in their hands; And cried with a loud voice, saying, Salvation to our God which sitteth upon the throne, and unto the Lamb.
– Revelation 7:9-10

Those saved, before the coming of Christ, could be numbered as we learn from the context.

John had a wonderful vision; he saw the outcome of the old and new dispensations.

We must not construe the context in a literal way to mean only one hundred and forty-four thousand, but the fact taught that those saved before the coming of Christ could be counted.

1. THEIR COMPANY IS GREAT

"a great multitude, which no man could number."

    1) Because a large number of humanity dies in infancy.

      "I take these little lambs," said he,
        "And lay them in my breast;
        Protection they shall find in me,
          In me be ever blest.
        Death may the bands of life unloose,
          But can't dissolve my love;
        Millions of infant souls compose
          The family above."

2) Because of the continued power of the Gospel to save to the end of time. The day will come when *"the earth shall be full of the knowledge of the Lord as the waters cover the sea."* (Isa. 11:9). We are, perhaps, only in the twilight of that glorious day when all shall know Him from the least unto the greatest.

2. THEIR NAMES ARE KNOWN

1) "All nations," etc.

2) " Kindreds." We shall know our loved ones in glory.

3. THEIR POSITION IS EXALTED

1) Christ had promised, *"where I am, there ye may be also"* (John 3:3).

2) Here is the fulfillment, *"stood before the throne and before the Lamb."*

4. THEIR SHOUT IS TRIUMPHANT

They gave all the praise to God and the Lamb for their cleansing, indicated by "white robes"; and their victory over sin, sorrow, sickness, death, and the grave, indicated by the expression, "palms in their hands."

Was your departed loved one a true Christian? It was by the value of His atoning blood and the cleansing power of the Holy Spirit that he was prepared to enter that grand assembly. He is now beyond the reach of sin and death. He is now with the pure and good of all who have gone. He is not dead; he lives in the highest sense.

Do you desire to meet him? Then trust in the Savior of men. There is no other way.

13. THE FUTURE STATE

And God shall wipe away all tears from their eyes; and there shall be no more death, neither sorrow, nor crying, neither shall there be any more pain: for the former things are passed away. – Revelation 21:4

Death suggests questions about the world beyond. The Old Testament answers, but they are often vague and unsatisfactory. The New Testament is more satisfactory. Paul gives a brief description of the celestial body and some of the conditions of the heavenly world. John, in the Revelation, presents some pictures of the heavenly place. From scriptural teaching we learn several characteristics of the future state.

1. THERE IS FREEDOM FROM PAIN

"neither shall there be any more pain."

We are acquainted with pain brought on by sickness and other incidents of our physical and social relations. We hunger and thirst on account of the want of worldly possessions and the loss of friends. We can rest in this promise:

They shall hunger no more, neither thirst any more. – Revelation 7:16

2. THERE IS EXEMPTION FROM DEATH

"there shall be no more death."

Here we are in the world of the dying. Our loved ones are snatched away and in regard to our own life we do not know what a day may bring forth. In the future state "there shall be no more death." The everlasting life given to believers through Christ cannot be broken by any power. The river and tree of life will afford a never-ending sustenance.

3. THERE IS GODLY COMPANIONSHIP

The average human being craves companionship. There must be common interests and similar dispositions to afford complete fellowship. It is imperfect here. In the future state we shall enjoy the society of the redeemed people of earth, the angels of light, and the Great God and Redeemer. Having been cleansed from earthly impurity we shall be like the other inhabitants of heaven, and, therefore, in harmony with our surroundings.

4. THERE IS PERFECT KNOWLEDGE

Here we are annoyed because we know only in part and see through a glass darkly. In the future world we shall know as we are known and enjoy the blessings of knowledge that is free from earthly limitations.

For now we see through a glass, darkly; but then face to face: now I know in part; but then shall I know even as also I am known. – 1 Corinthians 13:12

14. SEVEN TRUTHS FOR THE BELIEVER IN PSALM 23:4

Yea, though I walk through the valley of the shadow of death, I will fear no evil: for thou art with me; thy rod and thy staff they comfort me. – Psalm 23:4

1. HIS PLACE

The valley of the shadow of death.

2. HIS PROGRESS

Walk.

3. HIS PEACE

Fear no evil.

4. HIS PERSONAL COMPANION

Thou.

5. HIS PRESENCE

With me.

6. HIS PROTECTION

Thy rod and thy staff.

7. HIS PRESENT COMFORT

They comfort me.

15. THE BLESSEDNESS OF THE RIGHTEOUS

As for me, I will behold thy face in righteousness: I shall be satisfied, when I awake, with thy likeness. – Psalm 17:15

Three things offer themselves for our consideration today: Consider the nature of this blessedness.

1. THE VISION OF THE FACE OF GOD

1) The object of this vision: "Thy face."

(*a*) A sensible glory: such a glory was seen by Moses at Sinai, afterwards in the tabernacle, and at the transfiguration.

(*b*) An intellectual glory: Glory is resplendent excellency, real worth made conspicuous. This glory is the conspicuous luster of Divine perfections.

2) The act of beholding glory has a peculiar respect to the power of seeing. Sight is the most perfect sense; noble, comprehensive, quick, and energetic. The act of the mind is called seeing. The blessed shall have the glory of God so presented as "to know as they are known."

2. THE WAY WE PARTICIPATE IN HIS LIKENESS

How strange an errand the Gospel has in the world, to transform men and make them like God.

1) There is a sense in which we cannot be like God. God will endure no such imitation of Him as to be rivaled in the point of His Godhead (Ezek. 28:6-10.)

2) There is a just and admirable imitation of God: we are to be imitators of God (Eph. 5:1).

3) Man already has a likeness to God: the material world represents Him, as a house the builder; spiritual beings as a child the father: others carry his footsteps, these his image.

4) There is a natural image of God in the soul of man, inseparable from it, its spiritual immortal nature; its intellectual and elective powers are the image of the same powers of God. There is also a moral likeness, wisdom, mercy, truth, righteousness, holiness.

5) Assimilation to God in moral perfections conduces to the soul's satisfaction and blessedness: "We shall be like Him, for we shall see Him as He is." How great a hope is this! Were the dust of the earth turned into stars in the sky, what could equal the greatness and wonder of this mighty change.

3. THE RESULTING SATISFACTION

The soul's rest in God, its perfect enjoyment of the most perfect good, the perfecting of its desires in delight or joy. Desire is love in motion; delight, love in rest. It is a rational, voluntary, pleasant, active rest. It is the rest of hope perfected in fruition.

16. THE BRIGHT SIDE OF DEATH

Let me die the death of the righteous, and let my last end be like his! – Numbers 23:10b

There is a holy covetousness, and these words point to an illustrious example. We may covet love, sympathy, wisdom, holiness, usefulness, to die like the righteous, and entrance into heaven itself.

Most people look upon death as a dark and gloomy thing without one redeeming quality. But the death of the righteous, like the lowering clouds that shut out the sun at noonday, has a bright side and a silver lining.

1. DEATH IS SOMETHING WE SHRINK FROM

True to our natural instincts we shrink back from death.

With the Christian, as with Pascal, it is only the supposed pain of dying he fears. But the highest authority now declares that there is necessarily no pain in dying itself.

2. DEATH IS THE START OF ETERNITY

1) With the wicked, death is a final goodbye to all Gospel opportunities and holy companionships, and a plunge over the precipice of woe into the abysses of a starless night. With the Christian it is moving out into eternal daylight.

2) Much greater misfortunes than death can befall the Christian.

3. DEATH IS BRIEF AND TEMPORARY

Our intelligent and spiritual parts are essentially imperishable. Death does not destroy the inhabitant. It only takes down the house in which he lives. The faithful believer never dies.

And whosoever liveth and believeth in me shall never die. Believest thou this? – John 11:26

4. DEATH IS PUTTING ON IMMORTALITY

The grave is only an inn. Man was created immortal and he shall rise from the grave and live forever. Death shall be destroyed.

For this corruptible must put on incorruption, and this mortal must put on immortality. – 1 Corinthians 15:53

5. DEATH IS OUR ENTRANCE INTO HEAVEN

1) It is the soul's liberation from all bondage, and limitations that mar its larger pleasure and deter its expansion and unfolding. It is like the worm that bursts its chrysalis and comes forth a thing of larger life, liberty, and beauty.

2) It secures to the believer an immediate increase of all that is good in itself. It is going from large opportunities to larger ones. He is like one who moves from the poorhouse into king's palaces and from plain fare to everlasting banquets. It is departure from friends "to an innumerable company of angels," etc. Death is his last conflict for his crown. Amidst the shadows of the valley he shouts with Edward Payson, "The battle is fought and the victory is won."

3) It is recovery of and everlasting reunion with departed loved ones.

17. RELIEVING THOUGHTS CONCERNING DEATH

For I know that thou wilt bring me to death, and to the house appointed for all living. – Job 30:23

The text suggests some thoughts of Job concerning his own death. Every man must die, and every man may feel concerning his own death three things that have a tendency to make the soul calm, and even brave in the prospect:

1. THERE WILL BE NOTHING UNNATURAL IN MY DEATH

It is "appointed" as the death of every other kind of organized life on earth; it is the natural law of all organized bodies, to wear out, decay, and dissolve. As the earth takes back to itself all the elements that have entered into the composition of vegetables and animals, why should I refuse or dread the demand? I may rest assured that kind nature will make a benevolent and beneficent use of all the elements that have entered into my physical existence. Let me be ready to yield them up without reluctantance, ungrudgingly, thanking the Infinite for their use.

1) It is *dishonest* for me to object to this; for my body was only borrowed property, a temporary loan, nothing more.

2) It is *ungrateful* for me to object to this. Though I never had a claim to such a benefit, it has been of great service to my spiritual nature.

3) It is *unphilosophic* for me to object to this. Whatever my objections and resistance, it must come.

2. THERE WILL BE NOTHING UNCOMMON IN MY DEATH

"The house appointed for all living." Were I one of a few, amongst the millions of the race, singled out for such a destiny, I might complain; but since all, without any exception, must die, who am I that I should complain? Since Abraham and all the patriarchs, Isaiah and all the prophets, Paul and all the apostles, Luther and all the reformers, Milton and all the poets, Xavier and all the missionaries, up to the present period, have gone, why should I feel a moment's reluctance to join them in the mighty house? The fathers, where are they? and the prophets, do they live forever?

3. THERE WILL BE NOTHING ACCIDENTAL IN MY DEATH

"I know that Thou wilt bring me to death." I shall not die because of any fortuitous incident, or because of any fatalistic force, but because my Father brings me to the grave.

Thou prevailest for ever against him, and he passeth: thou changest his countenance, and sendest him away. – Job 14:20

There are no accidental deaths, no premature graves. The eternal, all-loving Father brings us to death, and for the Christian, it is a wonderful thing.

18. THE BLESSED DEAD

And I heard a voice from heaven saying unto me, Write, Blessed are the dead which die in the Lord from henceforth: Yea, saith the Spirit, that they may rest from their labours; and their works do follow them. – Revelation 14:13

In every other area of present existence, men's fortunes differ, but to die is common to all. The stream of life, whether it runs darkly or brightly, slowly or smoothly, is at last stopped by death. Other experiences may be escaped by various pleas, but there is no escape from the darkness of death that is coming upon all. It is inevitable, universal, and reasonable.

The text states a condition, describes a character, and assigns a reason.

1. THE CONDITION

"Blessed," *i.e.,* happy, satisfied, at peace, utmost capacity for happiness gratified. The Christian teaching, that death means more abundant life, sounds like a paradox. But if that is true, it is not peculiar to Christian faith. Everywhere life is conditioned by death. Every advance in life necessitates death. Nothing lives save as it extracts nourishment from air or water or earth, or from vegetable and animal tissues by a process which involves the decomposition of that on which it feeds.

2. THE CHARACTER

"Which die" in the Lord. The blessedness announced is the result of character and conduct, the character developed and made manifest by the conduct during life. They who cannot think cheerfully of death have probably never thought cheerfully and rationally of life. Those to whom death is a mysterious, and therefore, repugnant image, to such, life itself can be but a confused riddle, for they cannot as yet have any clear conception of the purpose of their existence. Life's great end is to make us like, and pleasing to, Christ. If life does this for us, we get the best out of it, and our life is completed, whatever the number of our days. Such a life is the only adequate preparation for a holy death, since the readiness for death is that of character, not of occupation.

3. THE REASON

"That they may rest from their labors; and their works do follow them."

1) Blessed in themselves, being at rest. The weariness of physical labor, the depressing reactions of intellectual pursuits, and the strain of spiritual conflict—all are things of the past.

2) Blessed in their reward. "Their works do follow them." While the price of their purchase and their title to Heaven absolutely and entirely involve, and depend upon, the blood of Christ, their works follow as the satisfactory evidence of having lived to, and died in, the Lord.

3) Blessed in their influence upon the living. While all their personal labor ends with life, the influence of that life remains with the living, so that, while dead, they still live. Observation and experience demonstrate that, long after they have passed away, the results of the life of the holy dead follow them.

Continuing, lasting power for good is the legacy to the world of all who "die in the Lord."

19. THOSE WHO DIE IN CHRIST

1. THOSE WHO DIE IN CHRIST POSSESS ETERNAL LIFE

And I give unto them eternal life; and they shall never perish, neither shall any man pluck them out of my hand. – John 10:28

2. THOSE WHO DIE IN CHRIST HAVE FOR A REFUGE AN ETERNAL GOD

The eternal God is thy refuge, and underneath are the everlasting arms: and he shall thrust out the enemy from before thee; and shall say, Destroy them. – Deuteronomy 33:27

3. THOSE WHO DIE IN CHRIST PRESS ON TOWARD AND ETERNAL INHERITANCE

And for this cause he is the mediator of the new testament, that by means of death, for the redemption of the transgressions that were under the first testament, they which are called might receive the promise of eternal inheritance. – Hebrews 9:15

4. THOSE WHO DIE IN CHRIST INHABIT AN ETERNAL HOUSE

For we know that if our earthly house of this tabernacle were dissolved, we have a building of God, an house not made with hands, eternal in the heavens. – 2 Corinthians 5:1

5. THOSE WHO DIE IN CHRIST WILL EXPER- IENCE AN ETERNAL WEIGHT OF GLORY

For our light affliction, which is but for a moment, worketh for us a far more exceeding and eternal weight of glory. – 2 Corinthians 4:17

6. THOSE WHO DIE IN CHRIST WILL SERVE AN ETERNAL KING

Now unto the King eternal, immortal, invisible, the only wise God, be honour and glory for ever and ever. Amen. – 1 Timothy 1:17

20. THE CHRISTIAN SERVANT ASLEEP

David, after he had served his own generation by the will of God, fell on sleep. – Acts 13:36a

David was a faithful worker, but his days were numbered. The time came when his labors were ended and God called him to his rest and his reward.

As with David so with all true Christians; their lives are spent in service, at length they fall asleep.

1. IT IS GOD'S WILL THAT HIS SERVANTS SLEEP

Our text teaches that he serves "by the will of God," it is equally true that "by the will of God" he sleeps. His work is appointed; when it is done God will cause him to lie down in the grave, which He has prepared as a bed of rest for all His faithful servants. He will issue His mandate, then "the dust shall return to the earth as it was" (Eccl. 12:7.)

2. WHEN SLEEP COMES WE CAN REST

Laid in the cemetery he is discharged from earthly service. He has run his race, has reached the goal, and has received the crown. He has fought his battles, vanquished his foes, and now exalts in victory. He has crossed life's ocean, experienced its storms and fogs, and now has entered the haven of everlasting rest.

3. WHEN WE SLEEP, WE SLEEP IN JESUS

United to Christ in life his dust is in union with Him in the grave. His sleep is sweet; sweeter than that of the baby lying on its mother's breast, than that of the laborer when his day's work is done.

4. WHEN WE SLEEP, WE STILL LIVE

The body may sleep and yet the mental and spiritual faculties be active. So in the case before us. Abraham, Isaac, and Jacob had been long asleep, yet Jesus taught they were living (Matt. 22:32). Moses fell asleep more than fourteen hundred years before the Christian era, yet he appeared on the Mount of Transfiguration and talked with Jesus.

5. WHEN WE SLEEP, WE KNOW WE WILL AWAKE

The night shall terminate, the morning dawn. The Master will call him at the set time, then he shall rise reinvigorated, refreshed, ready for new service. He shall awake never to sleep again.

> 1) *Let tired laborers be encouraged.* There is a time of rest.

> 2) *Let mourners be comforted.* Your loved ones, who served the Savior, are only sleeping. They shall awake to newness of life.

21. THE LOSS OF A CHILD

But now he is dead, wherefore should I fast? can I bring him back again? I shall go to him, but he shall not return to me. – 2 Samuel 12:23

The context shows David in two aspects. First: *Suffering as a sinner.* He had committed a great sin, and the loss of his child was retribution. Secondly: *Reasoning as a saint.* *"And he said, While the child was yet alive, I fasted and wept: for I said, Who can tell whether God will be gracious to me, that the child may live? But now he is dead, wherefore should I fast? can I bring him back again? I shall go to him, but he shall not return to me."* The text implies David's belief in three things.

1. THE SEPARATION OF DEATH

"He shall not return to me." He felt that all grief was useless, all prayer was unavailing. The dead do not return again.

When a few years are come, then I shall go the way whence I shall not return. – Job 16:22

Hezekiah said: *"I shall behold man no more with the inhabitants of the world."* – Isaiah 38:11

> 1) *There is no returning to take care of neglected duties.* Duties which we have neglected in relation to our children, our friends, our neighbors, our country, we can never return after to discharge. They remain undone.

> 2) *There is no returning to recover lost opportunities.* Lost Sundays, lost sermons, lost means of grace, no one comes back from the grave

to redeem. If there is no return to the earth—How foolish is it to set our hearts upon it, and how important to finish its work as we go on. The text implies David's belief in—

2. THE CERTAINTY OF DEATH

"I shall go to him." He had no doubt on the subject, nor has anyone any reason to doubt. *"It is appointed unto all men once to die." "One generation cometh, and another passeth away." "We must all die, and be as water spilt upon the ground, which cannot be gathered up again."*

1) *The certainty of death is universally admitted.* There is no room left for questioning it. Death reigned from Adam to Moses, from Moses to Christ, from Christ to this hour.

2) *The certainty of death is universally denied by many in this life.* All men live as if they were immortal. How morally infatuated is our race! The good news is that the text implies David's belief in—

3. THE OVERCOMING OF DEATH

"I shall go to him."

But I would not have you to be ignorant, brethren, concerning them which are asleep, that ye sorrow not, even as others which have no hope. – 1 Thessalonians 4:13

1) *The reunion he believed in was spiritual.* It evidently means more than going to his grave, and the mingling of their dust together. There would be no consolation, in this.

2) *The reunion he believed in was conscious.* They would feel themselves together, recognize each other as child and father.

3) *The reunion he believed in was happy.* There would be no consolation in the idea of an unhappy union. He believed that his child was happy. Infants go to heaven. *"Of such,"* says Christ, *"is the kingdom of heaven."* He believed that he was safe. He felt that he should go to him, and be with him in that happy world.

22. THE DEATH OF THE SAINTS OF GOD

1. THEY ARE GOD'S POSSESSION

Who gave himself for us, that he might redeem us from all iniquity, and purify unto himself a peculiar people, zealous of good works. – Titus 2:14

2. THEY ARE READY FOR HEAVEN

Giving thanks unto the Father, which hath made us meet to be partakers of the inheritance of the saints in light. – Colossians 1:12

3. THEY ARE MARKED WITH GOD'S SEAL

And grieve not the holy Spirit of God, whereby ye are sealed unto the day of redemption. – Ephesians 4:30

4. THEY ARE BROUGHT TO THEIR HAVEN

Then are they glad because they be quiet; so he bringeth them unto their desired haven. – Psalm 107:30

5. THEY ARE SLEEPING IN JESUS

For if we believe that Jesus died and rose again, even so them also which <u>sleep in Jesus</u> will God bring with him. – 1 Thessalonians 4:14

6. THEY ARE BROUGHT WITH CHRIST

For if we believe that Jesus died and rose again, even so them also which sleep in Jesus will <u>God bring with him</u>. – 1 Thessalonians 4:14

23. HEAVEN A BETTER COUNTRY

But now they desire a better country, that is, an heavenly: wherefore God is not ashamed to be called their God: for he hath prepared for them a city. – Hebrews 11:16

The text refers to the believing patriarchs described in the former part of the chapter; but is equally applicable to all who count themselves strangers and pilgrims on the earth, and who are traveling in the way to the heavenly Zion.

1. THE "COUNTRY" CALLED "HEAVEN"

"A better country, that is, heavenly." Sometimes heaven is described as a city—a kingdom—a temple—an inheritance. In the text it is called a country, doubtless in allusion to the country of Canaan, which was a striking type of the heavenly rest. This heavenly country is only partially revealed to us. Perhaps at present we are not capable of knowing much of its nature, etc. In the text it is, however, stated to be "a better country," better, infinitely better, than the present world. It is better because:

1) *It is a more exalted country.* The most glorious part of the creation. Where the God of hosts has His palace—throne—court, etc. The heaven of heavens. Full of the the divine glory.

2) *It is a more holy country.* Not polluted. No sin within its happy lands.

3) *It is a more healthy country.* Sin is the cause of disease; therefore, as there is no sin, there is no curse. No bodily, no mental, no spiritual afflictions are there.

4) *It is a more happy country.* Sources of grief and pain, are not feared and unknown. No seeds of bitterness—no crosses—open foes—false friends—imperfect brethren—no poverty—nor sorrows—nor toil—no fears—no temptation—no death.

5) *It is a more abiding country.* Not to be visitors but residents. Not visitors for a season, but inhabitants forever. That inheritance is incorruptible—that crown does not fade—that kingdom is an everlasting kingdom.

6) *It is a better country, as it is the place of perfection and absolute glory.*

Perfect capacities—perfect enjoyment—perfect security—perfect employment—perfect day. Unclouded light. The height of glory. Bliss unchanging and unchangeable.

2. THE COUNTRY ALL BELIEVERS DESIRE

1) *We have secured a title to it.* By faith in Christ Jesus we are accepted of God, are His children, and, if children, then *heirs,* etc. "Begotten again to a lively hope," etc. Names written in heaven.

2) *We are longing to enjoy it.* That better country is a heavenly one. It is necessary, therefore, that we be heavenly. Born from above. Heavenly nature. Heavenly dispositions. Heavenly conversation, etc.

3) *We labor and pray for it.* We express our desires to God. Seek grace to enable us to travel onward until we appear perfect before the God of gods in Zion.

4) *We talk of it, and live in the hope of its eternal enjoyment.* We seek the company of heaven-bound travelers. Speak of the glories of that kingdom. And our souls glow with the hope of dwelling in it forever and ever.

24. WHAT WE KNOW

1. WE KNOW HE ABIDES IN US

And he that keepeth his commandments dwelleth in him, and he in him. And hereby we know that he abideth in us, by the Spirit which he hath given us. – 1 John 3:24

2. WE KNOW WE HAVE A BUILDING OF GOD

For we know that if our earthly house of this tabernacle were dissolved, we have a building of God, an house not made with hands, eternal in the heavens. – 2 Corinthians 5:1

3. WE KNOW WE ARE OF THE TRUTH

And hereby we know that we are of the truth, and shall assure our hearts before him. – 1 John 3:19

4. WE KNOW THE SON OF GOD HAS COME

He that believeth on the Son of God hath the witness in himself: he that believeth not God hath made him a liar; because he believeth not the record that God gave of his Son. – 1 John 5:10

5. WE KNOW IT IS THE LAST TIME

Little children, it is the last time: and as ye have heard that antichrist shall come, even now are there many antichrists; whereby we know that it is the last time. – 1 John 2:18

6. WE KNOW WE HAVE PASSED OUT OF DEATH INTO LIFE

We know that we have passed from death unto life, because we love the brethren. He that loveth not his brother abideth in death. – 1 John 3:14

7. WE KNOW WE SHALL BE LIKE HIM

Beloved, now are we the sons of God, and it doth not yet appear what we shall be: but we know that, when he shall appear, we shall be like him; for we shall see him as he is.
– 1 John 3:2

25. THE GATES OF DEATH

Have the gates of death been opened unto thee? or hast thou seen the doors of the shadow of death? – Job 38:17

We have been in the presence of death. We stand beside the mortality of one to whom the gates of death have been opened to let her soul pass within. They open inward, and constantly they swing to receive the parting souls.

1. DEATH IS A MYSTERY BECAUSE LIFE IS A MYSTERY

1) No one has ever seen life itself. Its secret is hidden with God. Scientists are searching for life, but cannot find it.

2) No one has ever seen life itself leave the body. We know a life only as contained in a living body, death only as the opposite of a living body.

2. DEATH WILL ALWAYS BE A MYSTERY TO AN UNBELIEVER

1) Accepting no revelation from the Spirit all spiritual things must be unknown quantities.

2) Death is a thing of the spirit, because the material body is practically the same immediately before death or immediately after.

3) Death is a recognized fact, an unaccounted for fact, hence a mystery.

3. DEATH IS NO LONGER A MYSTERY TO THE BELIEVER

1) One has opened the gates of death outward and returned to tell us of death.

2) He taught us of death while still living.

3) The things within the gates of death have been revealed to us by the inspiration of God through the apostles.

Sympathy for the grieving is deep and heartfelt, assurance of her welfare and her gain cannot be questioned. Her life of faith and service terminated joyously, and her death, like the sun breaking through a storm cloud at the close of day, gave promise for the beautiful tomorrow, beyond clouds, storm, or suffering.

26. THE INEVITABILITY OF DEATH

For the living know that they shall die. – Ecclesiastes 9:5a

Life is but a short journey from the cradle to the tomb; and death, with its concrete finality, must be experienced by men and women of all nations.

1. WHAT IS IMPLIED IN DYING?

The question is bold, and cannot be fully answered; for the living have not experienced it, and the dead do not reveal the profound secret. Some suppose that it implies an utter extinction of being; but they neither regard the dictates of reason, nor the discoveries of revelation, both of which proclaim the soul of man immortal.

> 1) Death implies *a separation of soul and body.* Man is a compound being, of body and soul, of matter and spirit. His body is of the dust; his soul is from God. These are mysteriously united; but death dissolves the union, and breaks the unknown tie.
>
> *Then shall the dust return to the earth as it was: and the spirit shall return unto God who gave it.* – Ecclesiastes 12:7
>
> 2) Another thing implied in death is, *a final departure out of this world.*
>
> *For here have we no continuing city, but we seek one to come.* – Hebrews 13:14
>
> 3) The last thing implied in death is, *an entrance unto a new state of existence.*

2. HOW DO THE LIVING KNOW THEY WILL DIE?

The living know, *by the appointment of God,* that they will die.

1) The *death of others* is a proof that we must die. Men are dying daily and hourly. Perhaps there is not a moment in which some are not passing out of time into eternity.

2) We know we will die *by what we feel in ourselves.* Every pain we feel, every degree of weariness and weakness, proclaims the approach of death.

3. WHAT CAN WE DO TO MAKE DYING A POSITIVE EXPERIENCE?

1) We can *improve the present life* through which we pass. Then, when we come to reflect, in the hour of death, upon our conduct in life, we shall have cause to bless God for that grace which has enabled us to do His blessed will.

2) *Our sins should die before us,* so that they do not sink us lower than the grave. Death destroys the body; but it cannot destroy sin.

3) Let us earnestly *seek that spiritual life,* which cannot be destroyed by death. That person who is spiritually alive, may look at death with boldness, and bid defiance to its utmost rage. He has nothing to fear. God is with him. Angels wait to take him to the regions of immortality. And even his perishing body will rise again, to die no more. *Amen.*

27. AN AGED PILGRIM'S DEPARTURE

1. CALLED BY GOD AT THE BEGINNING

Now the LORD had said unto Abram, Get thee out of thy country, and from thy kindred, and from thy father's house, unto a land that I will shew thee: And I will make of thee a great nation, and I will bless thee, and make thy name great; and thou shalt be a blessing. – Genesis 12:1-2

2. OBEYED THE CALL OF FAITH

By faith Abraham, when he was called to go out into a place which he should after receive for an inheritance, obeyed; and he went out, not knowing whither he went. – Hebrews 11:8

3. WAS JUSTIFIED BY BELIEVING

For what saith the scripture? Abraham believed God, and it was counted unto him for righteousness. – Romans 4:3

4. ENJOYED THE FRIENDSHIP OF GOD

And the scripture was fulfilled which saith, Abraham believed God, and it was imputed unto him for righteousness: and he was called the Friend of God. – James 2:23

5. LOOKED FOR THE CITY OF GOD

For he looked for a city which hath foundations, whose builder and maker is God. – Hebrews 11:10

6. WENT TO BE WITH GOD

I am the God of Abraham, and the God of Isaac, and the God of Jacob? God is not the God of the dead, but of the living. – Matthew 22:32

28. THE IMPORTANCE OF PREPARATION

Watch ye therefore: for ye know not when the master of the house cometh, at even, or at midnight, or at the cockcrowing, or in the morning: Lest coming suddenly he find you sleeping. – Mark 13:35-36

The great lesson for us to learn from this text is that we should always be ready for death. This tabernacle must be dissolved. We should be ready for that event. Since so much has been done for man, preparation is possible. If preparation is not made, the results will be sad. If the soul is prepared, the results will be magnificent.

1. PREPARATION IS POSSIBLE

1) Provisions have been made for our instruction.

(a) Nature's light; *(b)* Bible; *(c)* Holy Spirit; *(d)* Ministry of angels; *(e)* Ministry of good people.

2) Provisions have been made for our cleansing.

Blood of Christ.

3) Provisions have been made for our spiritual development.

Laws of growth (conditions can be complied with).

2. PREPARATION MUST NOT BE NEGLECTED

1) Death is a sad event for those who neglect their soul.

2) His condition is miserable – "Weeping and wailing and gnashing of teeth"—Pangs of a guilty conscience—Remembrance of (a) Great salvation

neglected; (b) Good that might have been done; (c) That his condition might have been better.

3) He finds himself unfit for Heaven.

(a) Impure; (b) Not prepared for the higher service; (c) Not in harmony with celestial surroundings (no kindred spirit there).

4.)A hopeless state—No second chance—Lost forever.

3. PREPARATION RESULTS IN GLORY

1) Death for the Christian is a wonderful event. Beautiful scenes meet his eye—A glorified Christ—A beautiful home—Saints in glory.

2) Death for the Christian brings joy. Fullness of joy—Perfect peace—Endless bliss.

3) When a Christian dies he finds himself prepared for heaven. The preparatory course has been taken (a) Prepared for higher service (b) In harmony with celestial surroundings (c) Finds kindred spirits there—Heaven is home for the saints.

How careful we should live, ever seeking that preparation that is necessary. Nothing else can take its place. No grand funeral nor eloquent funeral address by some eloquent speaker, nor flattering obituary written by some friend, can take the place of that preparation that should have been made.

29. THE BELIEVER'S RICHES IN GLORY

1. A SAVIOR IN HEAVEN

For our conversation is in heaven; from whence also we look for the Saviour, the Lord Jesus Christ. – Philippians 3:20

2. A SURE HOPE

For the hope which is laid up for you in heaven, whereof ye heard before in the word of the truth of the gospel. – Colossians 1:5

Which hope we have as an anchor of the soul, both sure and stedfast, and which entereth into that within the veil. – Hebrews 6:19

3. A LIFE HIDDEN WITH CHRIST

If ye then be risen with Christ, seek those things which are above, where Christ sitteth on the right hand of God. Set your affection on things above, not on things on the earth. For ye are dead, and your life is hid with Christ in God. – Colossians 3:1-3

And hath raised us up together, and made us sit together in heavenly places in Christ Jesus. – Ephesians 2:6

4. A HEAVENLY CITIZENSHIP

For our conversation ("citizenship") is in heaven; from whence also we look for the Saviour, the Lord Jesus Christ. – Philippians 3:20

5. A GREAT HIGH PRIEST

Seeing then that we have a great high priest, that is passed into the heavens, Jesus the Son of God, let us hold fast our profession. – Hebrews 4:14

6. AN INHERITANCE

To an inheritance incorruptible, and undefiled, and that fadeth not away, reserved in heaven for you. – 1 Peter 1:4

7. A NAME WRITTEN IN HEAVEN

Notwithstanding in this rejoice not, that the spirits are subject unto you; but rather rejoice, because your names are written in heaven. – Luke 10:20

8. A TREASURE WAITING

But lay up for yourselves treasures in heaven, where neither moth nor rust doth corrupt, and where thieves do not break through nor steal. – Matthew 6:20

9. A MASTER

And, ye masters, do the same things unto them, forbearing threatening: knowing that your Master also is in heaven; neither is there respect of persons with him. – Ephesians 6:9

10. A FATHER

Let your light so shine before men, that they may see your good works, and glorify your Father which is in heaven. – Matthew 5:16

Jesus saith unto her, Touch me not; for I am not yet ascended to my Father: but go to my brethren, and say unto them, I ascend unto my Father, and your Father; and to my God, and your God. – John 20:17

30. SLEEP IN JESUS

For if we believe that Jesus died and rose again, even so them also which sleep in Jesus will God bring with him. –
1 Thessalonians 4:14

> "Salvation, O the joyful sound,
>   What pleasure to our ears!
> A sovereign balm for every wound,
>   A cordial for our fears."

Yes, this is the glory of the Gospel, that it completely meets the condition and need of the sinner. Man is guilty, and it reveals forgiveness; man is an alien, and it brings him back to the divine family; man is unholy, and it regenerates and sanctifies him; man is wretched, and it imparts abiding peace; man is dying, and it reveals to him a better world; man is destined to be the resident of the dust, and it throws its celestial radiance across the tomb;— and addresses us:

But I would not have you to be ignorant, brethren, concerning them which are asleep, that ye sorrow not, even as others which have no hope. For if we believe that Jesus died and rose again, even so them also which sleep in Jesus will God bring with him. – 1 Thessalonians 4:13-14

1. IN THE BIBLE, DEATH IS DESCRIBED AS "SLEEP"

"Sleep." The idea is very commonly presented to us in the Bible. The metaphor of sleep represents death,

> 1) As a state of rest. And this is a perfect contrast to the state of the Christian in life. Now, he is a servant, and has to toil in the vineyard of Christ. But

then the master says, It is enough; "well done, good and faithful servant."

2) A state of unconsciousness. In sleep, the avenues of the senses are closed. "We see not—we hear not," etc. We are unaware to all events which surround us. So in death, we are strangers to all that is done beneath the sun.

His sons come to honour, and he knoweth it not; and they are brought low, but he perceiveth it not of them. – Job 14:21

3) As a temporary state. A few hours' sleep and it is over. So death has not the sign of permanence upon it. It will only detain us one short-lived night, and then be over forever.

2. FOR THE CHRISTIAN, DEATH IS DESCRIBED AS "SLEEP IN JESUS"

They "which sleep in Jesus." Now, this implies,

1) That they have been united to Christ in life in salvation.

2) It implies that they have died in Christ, as well as lived in Him.

3) To sleep in Jesus implies that they sleep in the personal certain hope of an interest in all Christ has obtained for them

3. GOD PROMISES TO BRING THOSE WHO SLEEP IN JESUS "WITH HIM"

The subject refers to Christ's Second Coming. Then will Jesus raise His saints, and they will ascend with Him, as

His illustrious train; and so be forever with the Lord. Those who sleep in Jesus:

> 1) Will have a part in the first resurrection. "Christ, the first-fruits," etc (1 Cor. 15:23). "Blessed and holy are they who have," etc (Rev. 20:6). "The upright shall have dominion over them in the morning" (Psalm 49:14).

> 2) They shall possess the glorious image of Jesus.

> *For our conversation is in heaven; from whence also we look for the Saviour, the Lord Jesus Christ: Who shall change our vile body, that it may be fashioned like unto his glorious body, according to the working whereby he is able even to subdue all things unto himself.* – Philippians 3:20-21

> 3) They shall be coheirs with Christ forever and ever.

> *And if children, then heirs; heirs of God, and joint-heirs with Christ; if so be that we suffer with him, that we may be also glorified together.* – Romans 8:17

31. FROM POVERTY TO POVERTY

For we brought nothing into this world, and it is certain we can carry nothing out. – 1 Timothy 6:7

1. WE BROUGHT NOTHING INTO THIS WORLD

We brought no property into this world. We brought no accomplishments into this world. All we brought was the mind of an infant.

And said, Naked came I out of my mother's womb, and naked shall I return thither: the LORD gave, and the LORD hath taken away; blessed be the name of the LORD. – Job 1:21

However, we did bring:
> 1) A capacity for impressions
> 2) A capacity for imitations
> 3) Inherited tendencies
> 4) Self-determination

2. WE CAN TAKE NOTHING OUT OF THIS WORLD

For when he dieth he shall carry nothing away: his glory shall not descend after him. – Psalm 49:17

We cannot carry out any property or possessions. But we do take with us:
> 1) Our character
> 2) Our memories
> 3) Our rewards
> 4) Our faith

32. CHRIST, THE RESURRECTION AND THE LIFE

Jesus said unto her, I am the resurrection, and the life: he that believeth in me, though he were dead, yet shall he live: And whosoever liveth and believeth in me shall never die. Believest thou this? – John 11:25-26

In the history before us we have an account of a heavy affliction that had befallen a family, through the death of one to whom Jesus had shown a very peculiar attachment. He had been asked to come and help them, but He had delayed His visit till the sick person had been dead four days. This He had done intentionally, in order that He might demonstrate more fully to the grieving sisters His own power and glory. Accordingly, when they stated that, if He would pray to God for the restoration of their brother to life, God would grant His request, He told them that He did not need to implore God for this because He Himself was the resurrection and the life, and was able to impart either bodily or spiritual life to anyone He chose.

In considering this most remarkable declaration, we notice:

1. JESUS IS THE RESURRECTION

Martha expressed her expectation of a general resurrection at the last day. Jesus replied to her:

"I am the resurrection." He identified Himself personally with the act of resurrection.

Our Lord, in His divine nature, possessed omnipotence, necessarily, and of Himself.

"I am the life."

In this term our Lord proceeds further than in the first statement, and asserts, that as He is the author and first-fruits of the resurrection, so He is the very principle of life whereby His people live.

2. JESUS WILL RAISE HIS FOLLOWERS FROM THE DEAD

There is a remarkable correspondence between the two latter and the two former clauses of the text; the latter declaring the operation of the powers expressed in the former.

1) Being *"the resurrection,"* He will raise the bodies of his people.

2) Being *"the life,"* He will preserve the souls of His people unto everlasting life.

33. THROUGH JESUS

For of him, and through him, and to him, are all things: to whom be glory for ever. Amen. – Romans 11:36

1. (Name of deceased) HAS PEACE WITH GOD THROUGH OUR LORD JESUS CHRIST

Therefore being justified by faith, we have peace with God through our Lord Jesus Christ. – Romans 5:1

2. (Name of deceased) HAS JOY IN GOD THROUGH OUR LORD JESUS CHRIST

And not only so, but <u>we also joy in God through our Lord Jesus Christ</u>, by whom we have now received the atonement. – Romans 5:11

3. (Name of deceased) HAS RECEIVED THE ATONEMENT THROUGH OUR LORD JESUS CHRIST

And not only so, but we also joy in God through <u>our Lord Jesus Christ, by whom we have now received the atonement</u>. – Romans 5:11

4. (Name of deceased) HAS ETERNAL LIFE THROUGH OUR LORD JESUS CHRIST

For the wages of sin is death; but the gift of God is eternal life through Jesus Christ our Lord. – Romans 6:23

5. (Name of deceased) HAS VICTORY OVER DEATH THROUGH OUR LORD JESUS CHRIST

But thanks be to God, which giveth us the victory through our Lord Jesus Christ. – 1 Corinthians 15:57

34. THE STONE ROLLED AWAY

And, behold, there was a great earthquake: for the angel of the Lord descended from heaven, and came and rolled back the stone from the door, and sat upon it. – Matthew 28:2

It is probable that Christ arose at dawn, through the sealed stone, and that the angel descended "at the rising of the sun," when the women approached the sepulcher, and rolled back the stone to show them that Christ was risen.

When Jesus Rose:

1. SIN WAS ROLLED AWAY

Before Christ's death and resurrection the condition of sinful man was deplorable. His iniquities weighed him down, there was no remission of guilt; every sinful act plunged him deeper, and more irrevocably, in the mire of guilt. He could not shake off the burden of the past, and start afresh. The past with all its horrors lay on him, like the slab of the tomb. But now that is rolled away. "By the blood of the Covenant I have sent forth the prisoners out of the pit" (Zech. 9:11).

2. THE FEAR OF DEATH WAS ROLLED AWAY

This was the fear which, all their lifetime, held men in bondage; like the magnet mountain in the story, the attraction was irresistible, that drew men to death. Think of that fear! To count the pulsations of the heart, as the tick of the clock that draws towards termination. As a writer of old said, "Every stroke of my heart that I listen to at night, sounds to me as the ax of a woodman hacking down the tree of life." Think of the fear of death weighing night and day on man, never shaken off, a haunting dread when he lies down at night, when he wakes in the morning. Death feared, because what it leads to is unknown.

Goethe, when dying, said in an agitated voice, "What is coming? Oh, it is dark, it is dark!" Such is death to the unbeliever, uncertainty and gloom—the stone is on the tomb.

The last words of the late Bishop of Salisbury (Hamilton) were, "Oh, how bright!" with an indescribable smile—the stone was rolled away.

3. THE MISERY OF SEPARATION WAS ROLLED AWAY

What a bitter thing must have been the separation of the unbelieving father from his dying child, the husband from the wife. No hope. A look at the dear, dear face, so soon to be consigned to the dust. No prospect of seeing it again, nor of hearing the loved voice. All the old sweet affection stilled in that dead heart forever. An aching void, no hope to fill it, a blank future, no light to illumine it.

I sometimes wonder how a non-believer could survive the misery of parting with those dear to him.

But it is a different thing altogether to the Christian, the parting to him is only temporary, the prospect of meeting again is to him certain—so that this stone is rolled away.

Glory be to You O risen Savior, my hope, my desire, who has rolled away the stone of my sins, and the fear of death that oppressed me and who has given to me the hope, after this life ended, of meeting again those dear ones who have passed from my sight.

35. THE REST OF GOD'S PEOPLE

There remaineth therefore a rest to the people of God. – Hebrews   4:9

Let us labour therefore to enter into that rest, lest any man fall after the same example of unbelief. – Hebrews 4:11

All humankind are seeking something in which to find rest. The inquiry of so many is, "Who will show us any good?" Most seek it in the world, and seldom find anything except exasperation and disappointment. But the Bible reveals One who is willing to impart a lasting peace. The Savior says," Come unto me all ye that labor, and are heavy laden, and I will give you rest." The rest which Christ bestows in this world is comparative. It is more than its recipients once possessed; but it is not complete. It is only the foretaste of a fuller, a perfect rest. To this, the text refers, "There remaineth a rest to the people of God."

1. WHAT IS THE REST?

One very common notion of it is that it is an entire cessation from labor. To those who have been toiling all their lives, this is the prominent idea that it presents to the mind. But it is something more than this. The word translated "rest" certainly does denote a keeping of Sabbath. It is not a state of mere relaxation. As the Sabbath, a time set apart for God, brings its duties the noblest man can engage in on earth, so will this eternal Sabbath. The Sabbath among the Jews was peculiarly sacred. No secular work was allowed to be done on it. Toil was not permitted to defame it. The decalogue even forbid the use of the inferior animals, so that it might be a time of rest both for man and beasts. It was a day devoted exclusively to the Lord. So will this time be. It will be greater, because it is a perfect rest. The rest of God from the work of creation, the rest of man from worldly labor— these were foreshadowings and pledges of the eternal rest. In what will it specifically consist? It will be—

1) *A rest from sin.* It is for those who are purified from all that is evil. The unholy cannot possess it. They will not be allowed to partake of it. Nothing shall enter it that defiles, nothing that makes a lie.

2) *It will be a rest from sorrow.* This often comes to the Christian from the sins of others. When he is removed from these, he will have no more to trouble him. But these blessings are only negative. It consists of what is positive also.

(*a*) It is a bestowment of eternal life. This is the Christian's peculiar privilege. The Gospel has brought life and immortality to light.

(*b*) It is being with Christ. Now we see Him but by the eye of faith: then we shall see Him face to face.

(*c*) It is working for God without weariness, and with full power and ability to do so.

2. WHEN IS THE REST?

It is future. It is not a rest in this world. This life is a life of trouble and strife and toil. It is a period of discipline, and stern conflict. In it we work for the future, and upon it the future depends. Like a day of battle it will bring eternal peace, or unending bondage. It is true that this rest begins in this world. It commences with the renewed soul when it first "looks not at the things which are seen, but at the things which are not seen." It brightens upon us more and more as we rise from the lower, the temporal, to the higher, the eternal, life. It is fully revealed to us when we have done with mortality and sin. Until then we cannot completely enter into, nor enjoy, "the rest that remaineth for the people of God."

3. FOR WHOM IS THE REST?

They are a peculiar people. They are those who love holiness, and hate iniquity and sin. Their hearts are set to do right. Though in the world, they are not of the world. It is not for all men, because all will not receive it. They do not wish it. They will not obey God on earth; how could they serve Him in heaven? They hate the shadow of this rest. To some it is a weariness and a grief. They would willingly abolish it from the world. How, then, could they enjoy the substance?

To the one who neglects Christ, these words convey nothing but despair. There is a rest remaining, but it is not for him. Again and again he has been invited to the Savior, but he has preferred the things of the world to those of eternity. He casts realities away for shadows. Therefore he will have no part in this rest.

To the Christian, these words are full of hope and holy consolation. Weeping may endure for a night, but joy will come with the morning! The sins of the past may rise up in sorrow before him; but he has a rest that still remains. The world may be, and often is, a land of darkness and of the shadow of death; but he presses forward to a land of righteousness, of life, of light, of God.

36. THE VOICE FROM HEAVEN

And I heard a voice from heaven saying unto me, Write, Blessed are the dead which die in the Lord from henceforth: Yea, saith the Spirit, that they may rest from their labours; and their works do follow them. – Revelation 14:13

How much light dwells in this familiar sentence! How many truths gleam from it—gleam with all the varied beauty of the stones in the breastplate of the Hebrew priest of old! We have here:—

1. GOD'S CARE FOR THE GRIEVING

"I heard a voice from heaven"... "Saith the Spirit." The apostle was evidently thinking—a vision was passing before him that made the thought very vivid, of the persecution of the martyrs even unto death, and of the terrible havoc that the sharp sickle of death would work through the ages. While he is thinking of the death that would befall men, he is led to contemplate the voice and the writing of consolation. These come from heaven. Heaven cares for earth in its bitterest experiences. The Bible is full of this doctrine.

2. GOD'S RELATIONSHIP TO THOSE WHO DIE IN CHRIST

They "die in the Lord." They die, not merely believing in His teaching, not merely breathing His Spirit, but they die sustained by His grace and preserved by His power. The fellowship that Christian men and women had with Christ in their lifetime is not weakened or shaken by any of the mysterious experiences of death. Death rather intensifies and completes it.

3. GOD'S BLESSINGS TO THOSE WHO DIE IN CHRIST

That close relationship with Christ, in dying, has led to this fuller development of their blessedness. "Blessed are the dead." They are not to be thought of as those who have been taken over by some great adversary, and trampled down by some resistless foe. They are to be regarded as conquerors. That "rest!" What can it mean? It does not mean that they are gone out of being; for non-existence is not rest.

Death is not the end of the spirit-life. It is resting, not annihilated—resting, for it has returned to God who gave it. This rest is not a lapsing into some stagnant, weird inactivity. For it is equally true of those who are said to rest from their labors that "they rest not day nor night." These words cannot mean that we cease to think—cease to feel—cease to work after death. They indicate, surely, the fullness of life—the harmony of life—the complete satisfaction of life. They who have gone to heaven partake of this rest—the rest of Christ—the rest of God.

4. GOD'S INFLUENCE ON THOSE WHO DIE IN CHRIST

Dear to our loved one was many a project and plan born of love to Christ; very dear some accomplishments into which, in loving fellowship with others, they threw unreservedly their strength of body, and intellect, and heart. For their sake, as well as for our own and for Christ's, we rejoice to know that the seed they buried will spring up in rich harvests, that the sacred tones of their teachings will swell into growing harmonies—that the forces they set at work, however subtle and silent, will widen in influence and develop and multiply till myriads are affected by the life-work of one man. Lasting power for good is here described as the legacy to the world, not only of our reformers and authors and preachers, but of all whose Christly lives ended in a Christly death, and whose very death even, like their Lord's, was necessary to their deeper and wider and more sacred usefulness.

Verily, verily, I say unto you, Except a corn of wheat fall into the ground and die, it abideth alone: but if it die, it bringeth forth much fruit. – John 12:24

37. THE VICTORY OVER DEATH

The sting of death is sin; and the strength of sin is the law. But thanks be to God, which giveth us the victory through our Lord Jesus Christ. – 1 Corinthians 15:56-57

These words may be regarded as the summing up of Paul's argument concerning the resurrection of the dead. We will follow its thoughts in their order.

1. THE STING OF DEATH IS SIN

How true this is we all know. If our conscience did not condemn us and consequently give us an inkling of the judgment awaiting the sinful, death would have no sting, nothing of that venom which tortures and agonizes the soul in view of death, and that which follows death.

2. THE STRENGTH OF SIN IS THE LAW

Experience soon proves this declaration to be true. That which is unholy in us rises in rebellion against the assertion of God's holiness. Sin is pleasant, because forbidden, and makes that which forbids it, its occasion, its reason, in other words, its strength.

3. WE RECEIVE VICTORY THROUGH OUR LORD JESUS CHRIST

> 1) Because He proved that sin is not a necessary part of our humanity. He was holy, harmless, undefiled, and separate from sinners, though He was in all points tempted like as we are. To live as He lived are we exhorted, "because Christ also suffered for us, leaving us an example that we should follow His steps, who did no sin, neither was guile found in His mouth (1 Peter 2:21-22).

2) Because He gave Himself a sacrifice to redeem us from sin.

God made Him sin for us, who knew no sin, that we might be made the righteousness of God in Him (2 Cor. 5:21). He bare our sins in His own body on the tree, that we, being dead to sins, might live unto righteousness (1 Peter 2:24). Ye are bought with a price, therefore glorify God in your body and spirit which are God's (1 Cor. 6:20).

In this way Christ conquers sin in us. He makes us perfect in every good work to do His will. If we sin we repudiate that light and knowledge which enable us to see that the law is holy, and just, and good; and reject that wonderful and matchless love of God, who for us men and for our salvation sent His only begotten Son to live among us, so that we might know how to live, to die for us that we might reckon ourselves to be dead indeed unto sin, but alive unto God through Jesus Christ our Lord.

3) Because Christ was raised from the dead He gives us the victory over sin and death.

> *(a)* In this life we have a supernatural life through the death and resurrection of Christ.

> Paul says (Col. 3:1-2), "If ye then be risen with Christ, seek those things which are above, where Christ sitteth at the right hand of God. Set your affections on things above, not on things on the earth."

> *(b)* We also, if we believe in Him, have the assurance of resurrection unto glory.

Christ is risen from the dead, and become the first-fruits of them that slept. He says, "I go to prepare a place for you, and I will come again, and receive you unto myself, that where I am there ye may be also." So it is self-evident that when He shall appear, we shall be like Him, for we shall see Him as He is. Now every man that hath this hope in Him, purifieth himself, even as He is pure. Thus through Christ are we given victory over sin and death.

Therefore, my Christian friends, be steadfast in the faith of the resurrection. Unmovable in the assurance that the bodies of those who sleep in Him shall be raised at the last day, always abounding in the work of the Lord by keeping in subjection your bodies to holiness and living a life of faith on the son of God, who loved you, and gave Himself for you.

38. OUR RESURRECTION

Wilt thou shew wonders to the dead? shall the dead arise and praise thee? Selah. – Psalm 88:10

The great question of the human heart is, "Shall the dead arise and praise Thee?" or, as Job puts it, "If a man dies, shall he live again?" (Job 14:14). So every child of humanity often finds himself thinking on this question. After life here, what then? After death, what? Shall I pass into earth, into unconsciousness and unrecognition forever? Is death the end; or shall I rise again? Shall I live forever, shall I know and be known?

1. OUR RESURRECTION IS DESIRABLE

Man, everywhere and at all times, has desired to live after death. There is that in our nature that is not satisfied with the things of this life, but looks beyond to greater joys and happiness. This desire among all men has been given expression in the various views and creeds held by the different nations. We desire to live hereafter, because of friendships formed and love experienced here. These features of life which bring to the soul its chief joys, we would have continued forever. If in this life only we have hope in Christ, we are of all men most miserable.

2. OUR RESURRECTION IS POSSIBLE

If we are the result of certain forces in nature, we must be closely allied to nature and capable of its changes and phenomena. Our observation of nature's growth convinces us that its growth is made by certain kinds of deaths and resurrections. The harvest is the result of the dying grain. The natural law of life is death and renewal of life. Our resurrection is possible in God. He who created the body from nothing can renew the body in death. It is possible in Jesus Christ who conquered death and is able to give us the same conquering power. (See 1 Cor. 15:12-16).

3. OUR RESURRECTION IS CERTAIN

We desire it. God is able to raise us from the dead, and God will give us the desire of our hearts. Certain, because God's greatest glory is in man's resurrection; the effect of sin is death. Christ came to destroy the power of sin and death. This can be fully accomplished only in man's resurrection; therefore if there is no resurrection then Christ and God have failed. It is certain because Christ has promised it. "I will come again and receive you unto myself that where I am there ye may be also." So Paul is confident in proclaiming our resurrection in Christ. (See 1 Cor. 15:20-22).

Yes, it is certain, for

> If dull matter lives forever, why not mind and love so true?
> Surely these are things diviner than all else within the blue.
> Ever and forever singing, they go on their happy way;
> And shall love, God's best reflection, have its part within a day?
> All the spheres and all the ages, all the powers in the height
> Tell us naught e'er came to ruin save the wrongs that yield to right.
> Beauty, pleasure, mirth, and rapture, are they what they seem to be?

Faith and hope and love that figures in our life so
  constantly;
Surely these will last forever, for we know it should be
  so,
And what ought to be is certain while the cycles
  onward go.

The dead shall rise and praise God.

39. THE LAST STEP WE TAKE

And David sware moreover, and said, Thy father certainly knoweth that I have found grace in thine eyes; and he saith, Let not Jonathan know this, lest he be grieved: but truly as the LORD liveth, and as thy soul liveth, there is but a step between me and death. – 1 Samuel 20:3

1. IT IS A CERTAIN STEP

All must take it. Settle us in the finest spot in the most beautiful garden; let the fairest skies smile upon us, and the clearest streams wander by us; let us spend our time watching the flowers in spring, and listening to the bird's song; yet, even then, that step would appear before us: even then death would find us.

2. IT IS AN UNCERTAIN STEP

When we must take it we cannot tell. It may be tonight; it may be next week, or next year, or not for many years. When, we do not know. Where we must take it, is altogether hidden from us. It may be in the street or by the way; it may be in the house, or far away from friends and home. Where, is unknown to us.

3. IT IS A FINAL STEP

It is final because it puts an end to human distinctions. King and subject, prince and peasant, master and servant. It puts an end to the present character of human duties. The duties of parents and children, etc.

4. IT IS A PARTING STEP

It parts us from this world of matter. We must bid farewell to flower and star. It parts us from friends near and dear to us. It parts us from ourselves. That tender union that subsists between soul and body is rudely torn asunder; that body we have looked at so long, nourished and cherished so long, is left behind us when that step is taken.

5. IT IS A SOLITARY STEP

It is but one. Death is a lonely thing. We must take it all alone without friends. Unfortunately, some take it all alone without God!

6. IT IS A SOLEMN STEP

The step of birth is solemn. "It is an awful thing to be born," said one man, "because we have got into existence, and can never get out of it." The step of prayer is solemn. To bow in prayer before the throne of Him

"Who holds the universe
    Like a little fading flower,
That is worn upon His
    Garment for a little hour."

is surely solemn. No less solemn is the step of death, for it conducts us either downward into an unalterable and eternal hell, or upward into an unalterable and eternal heaven?

Prepare for taking this step. We should all desire to get to heaven at last. Then let us not forget that unless we repent and believe in Christ, except we are born again, all our cherished hopes of heaven will vanish like a vision, and leave nothing before us but the blackness of darkness forever.

40. NO TEARS IN HEAVEN

God shall wipe away all tears from their eyes; and there shall be no more death, neither sorrow, nor crying, neither shall there be any more pain: for the former things are passed away. – Revelation 21:4

1. THE TEARS WE HAVE ON EARTH

1) Tears are often caused by *temporary depression.* The laboring man weeps on account of the lack of things he has, or inadequate pay for labor—he weeps, too, as he feels his failing strength for his secular pursuits.

2) Tears arising from *defective relationships.* Some of these are very intimate, such as with close friends and loved ones. We've all shed tears over a relationship that did not turn out the way that we wanted.

3) *Tears caused by affliction.* How frail is the human frame! To what numerous diseases is it liable, the seeds of which are often in our genetics, and by external circumstances, ripen and bring forth fruit to death.

4) Tears are caused by *grief.* It is a solemn and an established fact that "we must needs die, and be as water spilt on the ground, which cannot be gathered up again," yet grief does violence to our feelings, and deeply pierces the hearts of survivors; for the relationships of life, generally speaking, are most tender and endearing, and more especially so when sanctified and refined by God's love.

5) *Many other causes of tears may be referred to.* The Christian weeps on account of his *moral imperfections.* He is weighed in the balance and found wanting.

2. THE ABSENCE OF TEARS IN HEAVEN

"God shall wipe away all tears from their eyes."

1) *Where?* In heaven—in God's own dwelling-place. In the Canaan above, where a tear was never yet shed, and never will be.

2) *Who shall wipe them away?* "*God* shall." Their removal is Divine. His infinite love to His people insures it. His infinite power will accomplish it. The immutability of His promise and oath to save to the uttermost, is the security for it.

3) *When will He do it?* "God *shall.*" It is future. He wipes away many tears in this world. He wipes away the tears of the repentant, and gives pardon and peace. He many times wipes away the tears of the afflicted, and brings them forth from the furnace like gold seven times purified. He wipes away the tears of adversity, and his Providence turns their mourning into joy.

4) *How will He do it?* "Shall *wipe away all tears.*"

(*a*) He will do it *affectionately.*

(*b*) He will do it *effectually;* "*all tears*" shall be "*wiped away.*" The cause shall be removed, and the effect shall cease.

(*c*) *He will certainly do it.* The language is positive. "God *shall.*" etc. The faith which believes it rests upon a Rock—the Rock of ages—the immutability of God. He will do exactly as He has promised.

The removal of tears implies the enjoyment of positive good. Instead of tears there will be joy—songs of triumph, and outbursts of gladness.

This freedom will be confined to God's people. Are you His?

How much we are indebted to Christ. He has entered heaven. He saves and prepares us for it.

How dreadful the prospect of the wicked! Their tears will never be wiped away.

41. NO NIGHT THERE

And there shall be no night there; and they need no candle, neither light of the sun; for the Lord God giveth them light: and they shall reign for ever and ever. – Revelation 22:5

It is impossible for us to conceive an exact idea of what Heaven will be like. It is one of God's designs that we shall not know on earth what He has "prepared for them that love Him." (See 1 Cor. 2:9.)

In this respect God acts as a Father to us. As a parent will not allow a child to see a birthday or a Christmas present until the day for its presentation arrives, so God, Who has prepared for them that love Him such good things as pass man's understanding, will not let them see those good things until the day of resurrection.

Yet He tells us something about Heaven. He tells us of many things which *will not be there.* There will be no more sea, no more curse, no more night. But let's consider the significance of the fact that "there shall be no night there."

It implies:

1. NO MORE SLEEP

Someone might object, and say there is no cause for satisfaction in this. The busy man, he would say, enjoys sleep. It is his refreshment after the labors of the day. Heaven would be none the better for having no time of rest.

We answer, in Heaven there will be nothing to make sleep either enjoyable or necessary. There will be *no more fatigue.* Yet, without sleep, in Heaven "the weary are at rest."

2. NO MORE SLEEPLESSNESS

Few things in life are so unpleasant as lying awake at night. It is one of the things that can sometimes make night dreadful. In Heaven there will be no sleeplessness, because there will be none of the problems which cause it: No sickness or sorrow; No anxiety; No anticipation of evil.

3. NO MORE FEAR

Timid people are frightened most easily at night. Men and women have been found dead after a night's confinement in a dark and lonely place. The darkness of night has this effect (in varying degrees according to the nervous temperament) on almost all people. Even good people are nervous and timid at night. Bad people are notably so. The conscience is an unpleasant companion in the dark.

In Heaven there will be no more fear.

4. NO MORE SIN

There is more sin of every kind committed at night than at any other time.

And this is the condemnation, that light is come into the world, and men loved darkness rather than light, because their deeds were evil. – John 3:19

For they that sleep sleep in the night; and they that be drunken are drunken in the night. – 1 Thessalonians 5:7

Into the land of eternal day "there shall in no wise enter any thing that defileth, neither whatsoever worketh abomination, or maketh a lie: but they that are written in the Lamb's book of life." (Rev. 21:27). In Heaven there shall be no more sin.

"And there shall be no night there; and they need no candle, neither light of the sun; for the Lord God giveth them light." Jesus, Who is the "Light of the world" now, will also be the Light of the "world to come."

John, who saw it, gave a record, saying:

And the city had no need of the sun, neither of the moon, to shine in it: for the glory of God did lighten it, and the Lamb is the light thereof. – Revelation 21:23

42. A SONG FOR THE SHADOWS

The LORD is my shepherd; I shall not want. He maketh me to lie down in green pastures: he leadeth me beside the still waters. He restoreth my soul: he leadeth me in the paths of righteousness for his name's sake. Yea, though I walk through the valley of the shadow of death, I will fear no evil: for thou art with me; thy rod and thy staff they comfort me. Thou preparest a table before me in the presence of mine enemies: thou anointest my head with oil; my cup runneth over. Surely goodness and mercy shall follow me all the days of my life: and I will dwell in the house of the LORD for ever. – Psalm 23:1-6

Henry Ward Beecher called the 23rd Psalm the *Nightingale Psalm*. He called it by this name because he said the nightingale sings its sweetest when the night is its darkest. He must have had in mind the words, "though I walk through the valley of the shadow of death, I will fear no evil; for thou art with me; thy rod and thy staff, they comfort me."

The valley of the shadow of death literally means the place of dark gloom or black darkness. It has references to any dark and gloomy experience of life through which we may have to travel. It is not limited exclusively to death, although it definitely includes it.

These experiences come to all people. Being a Christian doesn't exclude us from anything. Christians go bankrupt – Christians get cancer – Christians have accidents – And Christians die, just like everyone else.

Death comes to us all and to all those whom we love. And while having the Lord as our Shepherd grants us no immunity from sorrow, it does assure us of His presence,

His peace, and His promises. These are the things that enable us to sing even in the shadows of sorrow.

I believe it would be helpful for us in this hour if we could take a moment to consider:

1. GOD'S PRESENCE

The Psalmist writes, *"I will fear no evil: for thou art with me, thy rod and thy staff, they comfort me."*

Fear is in all probability the greatest enemy of mankind. And the fear of death is the greatest of all fears. As soon as people begin to love life, a fear of death is born. That is understandable. After all, death is an unknown – a mystery – and it seems so final.

But Christians do not need to be afraid of death, and we take comfort in the fact that our loved one is a Christian. We are assured that the Lord walks with us through the valley of the shadow. We are assured that He is here to comfort us. The Lord is so close to us that He shares our hurts, our feelings, and our pains. He enters into the depths of the experience w/us.

When our time comes to walk through the valley of the shadow of death, we can do it with calm assurance, for the Lord is with us – His rod and staff comfort us.

2. GOD'S PEACE

Thou preparest a table before me in the presence of mine enemies: thou anointest my head with oil; my cup runneth over. Surely goodness and mercy shall follow me all the days of my life.

With this verse the image changes from a pasture to a palace. God is no longer portrayed as the Good Shepherd. He is now the gracious host. In His presence hostility and strife are gone. We are at peace w/our enemies.

What is the enemy David is talking about? It is death – the last great enemy of man. And he is saying that even in the presence of death those who follow the Shepherd can have peace. This is the peace that our loved one is experiencing now.

Thou wilt keep him in perfect peace, whose mind is stayed on thee: because he trusteth in thee. – Isaiah 26:3

Peace I leave with you, my peace I give unto you: not as the world giveth, give I unto you. Let not your heart be troubled, neither let it be afraid. – John 14:27

And the peace of God, which passeth all understanding, shall keep your hearts and minds through Christ Jesus. – Philippians 4:7

It is only in the presence of the Shepherd that we can have calm assurance and peace in the hour of death.

3. GOD'S PROMISE

I will dwell in the house of the Lord forever.

The word "dwell" means to "settle down and be at home with." When we come to the end of our way, there is the prospect, the promise, that we will settle down and dwell at home with God forever.

This is the same promise that Jesus made when He said:

And they shall come from the east, and from the west, and from the north, and from the south, and shall sit down in the kingdom of God. – Luke 13:29

Beyond this life there is the Father's house. And it is pictured for us as a place for unbounded joy and unending goodness where we shall dwell forever.

When David wrote this Psalm, he had already seen tragedy, disappointment, heartache, and even death. But he had come to know the Lord as his Shepherd and he now lived w/confidence and assurance in Him. Out of that experience he gave us this song we can all sing in the dark shadows of sorrow. It is a song of God's Presence, God's Peace, and God's Promise.

43. DEATH SWALLOWED UP IN VICTORY

Now this I say, brethren, that flesh and blood cannot inherit the kingdom of God; neither doth corruption inherit incorruption. Behold, I shew you a mystery; We shall not all sleep, but we shall all be changed, In a moment, in the twinkling of an eye, at the last trump: for the trumpet shall sound, and the dead shall be raised incorruptible, and we shall be changed. For this corruptible must put on incorruption, and this mortal must put on immortality. So when this corruptible shall have put on incorruption, and this mortal shall have put on immortality, then shall be brought to pass the saying that is written, Death is swallowed up in victory. O death, where is thy sting? O grave, where is thy victory? The sting of death is sin; and the strength of sin is the law. But thanks be to God, which giveth us the victory through our Lord Jesus Christ. Therefore, my beloved brethren, be ye stedfast, unmoveable, always abounding in the work of the Lord, forasmuch as ye know that your labour is not in vain in the Lord. – 1 Corinthians 15:50-58

1. THE DECLARATION OF TRUTH

1) Something impossible announced. *"Now this I say, brethren, that flesh and blood cannot inherit the kingdom of God; neither doth corruption inherit incorruption."*

2) Something mysterious revealed. *"Behold I shew you a mystery; we shall not all sleep, but we shall all be changed."*

In addition to the general statement that all shall not sleep, but that all shall be changed, a peculiar feature is specified in reference to the resurrection of the dead, as well as the transformation of the living – namely, the fact that these great events take place instantaneously. The resurrection will be accomplished in less time than it takes us to pronounce the word. Oh, amazing thought! One moment the deep silence of the grave will be unbroken; its countless victims will be all lying in apparently eternal bonds: the next moment the trumpet sounds, and the reign of death is over. Every grave is empty, and each ocean cavern yields up its spoil.

And so with the transformation of the living. Both events will take place simultaneously.

2. THE FEELINGS OF TRIUMPH

"O death, where is thy sting? O grave, where is thy victory? The sting of death is sin: and the strength of sin is the law. But, thanks be to God, which giveth us the victory through our Lord Jesus Christ."

> 1) Forthcoming. Some regard these words as those of the saints on the great day. What they express will, doubtless, be their universal feeling: but it appears to be more natural to consider them as expressive of the apostle's own emotions, when, under the influence of that faith which brings distant objects near, the blissful consummation which he had been describing.

> 2) Often realized. In many a place where the Christian meets his fate, are the joyful strains heard, "O death, where is thy sting? O grave, where is thy victory?" The believer is a conqueror when he dies, as well as when he shall rise from the grave.

3) Intelligent. It is not a mere blind impulse, but its nature is understood. "The sting of death is sin; and the strength of sin is the law." It is by the extraction of its sting that the triumph over death is enjoyed.

4) Humbling. *"But, thanks be to God, which giveth us the victory through our Lord Jesus Christ."*

3. THE LIFE-CHANGING LESSONS

Therefore, my beloved brethren, be ye steadfast, unmoveable, always abounding in the work of the Lord, forasmuch as ye know that your labor is not in vain in the Lord.

1) Steadfastness. This has special reference to faith. When addressing the Colossians, the apostle says that he greatly rejoiced in beholding, "the steadfastness of their faith in Christ."

2) Immovability. This has reference to hope. We may have difficulties and temptations, but a hope so strong should inspire us with a full determination, in the divine strength, to hold on in the midst of all.

3) Abounding activity. *"Always abounding in the work of the Lord, forasmuch as ye know that your labor is not in vain in the Lord."*

44. THE CHRISTIAN FUTURE

And I heard a voice from heaven saying unto me, Write, Blessed are the dead which die in the Lord from henceforth: Yea, saith the Spirit, that they may rest from their labours; and their works do follow them. – Revelation 14:13

Reason and speculation can do but little towards removing the veil that hides from our view the mystery of the future. They can present nothing beyond feeble analogies and uncertain conjectures, which appear to be contradicted by many facts. But while reason has ever spoken with a feeble and faltering voice on the subject, the divine word has spoken with a positiveness that inspires confidence.

1. THIS REVELATION IS FROM HEAVEN

John tells us that he "heard a voice from heaven." (He was not listening to guesses of his own mind.) It was from heaven alone that any certainty could come. The voices of earth confuse and discourage faith.

2. THIS REVELATION IS OF PERMANENT VALUE

A mere voice might have died on the air, or even if its utterances had been conveyed from mouth to mouth during the first generations, they would have been in danger of distortion, but to make the views they give a permanent possession to all ages, John was commanded to write them.

3. THE REVELATION IS FULL OF COMFORT

It teaches us about the blessedness of those "who die in the Lord" and what it consists of. They are delivered from the trials and hardships of the present life. They shall "rest from their *labors*." Labor means strained and painful activity. This ceases in the blessed life. But the rest of God's saints is not described as a state of idleness, for we are told that "their works do follow them." They are still working in the line of their work here, but it is a work without toil, without friction, and blessed activity, which is the essential condition of true blessedness. Their work will be forever unimpeded and harmonious like a song without any jar or discord in it.

Such a heaven as this is in harmony with the laws of our nature—it depends on character, and it will consist in the free and unhindered exercise of our powers in the line of the holy desires which we cherish on earth. The heaven of the New Testament is a very different heaven from that we often hear described from some pulpits. It is a blessed state, because it is one of perfect rest, and it is a perfect rest because it activity without stress in the service we love on earth.

45. NOTABLE DAYS IN A PERSON'S HISTORY

1. THE DAY OF BIRTH

Man that is born of a woman is of few days, and full of trouble. – Job 14:1

2. THE DAY OF CONVERSION

And Jesus said unto him, This day is salvation come to this house, forsomuch as he also is a son of Abraham. – Luke 19:9

3. THE DAY OF DEATH

And he said, Behold now, I am old, I know not the day of my death. – Genesis 27:2

4. THE DAY OF RESURRECTION

Marvel not at this: for the hour is coming, in the which all that are in the graves shall hear his voice. – John 5:28

5. THE DAY OF JUDGMENT

Verily I say unto you, It shall be more tolerable for the land of Sodom and Gomorrha in the day of judgment, than for that city. – Matthew 10:15

46. THE REUNION TO COME

But I would not have you to be ignorant, brethren, concerning them which are asleep, that ye sorrow not, even as others which have no hope. For if we believe that Jesus died and rose again, even so them also which sleep in Jesus will God bring with him. For this we say unto you by the word of the Lord, that we which are alive and remain unto the coming of the Lord shall not prevent them which are asleep. For the Lord himself shall descend from heaven with a shout, with the voice of the archangel, and with the trump of God: and the dead in Christ shall rise first: Then we which are alive and remain shall be caught up together with them in the clouds, to meet the Lord in the air: and so shall we ever be with the Lord. Wherefore comfort one another with these words. – 1 Thessalonians 4:13-18

The Thessalonians had recently received the Gospel; and now some of their friends have died in the faith. As they expected to remain in the body until the Lord returned, and because some had fallen asleep through Jesus, they were troubled beyond measure. To counteract this tendency to focus on grief and trouble, the apostle consoles them with the pleasing hope of a happy and eternal reunion with the departed when the Lord appears in glory.

1. THERE WILL BE A REUNION

The dead have not perished. This separation will not be eternal. The departed will not lose anything. The living shall not precede the departed saints into the blessedness of eternal fellowship with Jesus (v.15. Both shall be caught up into the clouds and be with the Lord forever (v.17).

And then shall they see the Son of man coming in the clouds with great power and glory. – Mark 13:26

And if I go and prepare a place for you, I will come again, and receive you unto myself; that where I am, there ye may be also. – John 14:3

2. THIS REUNION IS BASED ON GOD'S PROMISES

This hope is built on a solid and indestructible foundation, because—

1) It is founded on the living Christ (v.14). The Lord's resurrection is the foundation of hope.

Blessed be the God and Father of our Lord Jesus Christ, which according to his abundant mercy hath begotten us again unto a lively hope by the resurrection of Jesus Christ from the dead. – 1 Peter 1:3

2) It is founded on the Lord's promised and expected return.

And to wait for his Son from heaven, whom he raised from the dead, even Jesus, which delivered us from the wrath to come. – 1 Thessalonians 1:10

And while they looked stedfastly toward heaven as he went up, behold, two men stood by them in white apparel; Which also said, Ye men of Galilee, why stand ye gazing up into heaven? this same Jesus, which is taken up from you into heaven, shall so come in like manner as ye have seen him go into heaven. – Acts 1:10-11

3. THIS REUNION WILL BE FULLY REALIZED

When the Lord visibly descends from heaven with great glory and power it shall be realized (v.16).

And then shall appear the sign of the Son of man in heaven: and then shall all the tribes of the earth mourn, and they shall see the Son of man coming in the clouds of heaven with power and great glory. And he shall send his angels with a great sound of a trumpet, and they shall gather together his elect from the four winds, from one end of heaven to the other. – Matthew 24:30-31

1) God will then bring the spirits of just men made perfect with Him (v.14).

And Enoch also, the seventh from Adam, prophesied of these, saying, Behold, the Lord cometh with ten thousands of his saints. – Jude 1:14

2) The dead raised (v.16). Before this promised reunion shall take place, the dead in Christ, must be raised with incorruptible, glorious, powerful, and spiritual bodies.

So also is the resurrection of the dead. It is sown in corruption; it is raised in incorruption: It is sown in dishonour; it is raised in glory: it is sown in weakness; it is raised in power: It is sown a natural body; it is raised a spiritual body. There is a natural body, and there is a spiritual body. – 1 Corinthians 15:42-44

3) And the living transformed. Then this final, happy, and eternal reunion and association of the living and dead shall be realized.

Behold, I shew you a mystery; We shall not all sleep, but we shall all be changed, In a moment, in the twinkling of an eye, at the last trump: for the trumpet shall sound, and the dead shall be raised incorruptible, and we shall be changed. For this corruptible must put on incorruption, and this mortal must put on immortality. So when this corruptible shall have put on incorruption, and this mortal shall have put on immortality, then shall be brought to pass the saying that is written, Death is swallowed up in victory. O death, where is thy sting? O grave, where is thy victory? The sting of death is sin; and the strength of sin is the law. But thanks be to God, which giveth us the victory through our Lord Jesus Christ. – 1 Corinthians 15:51-57

4. THIS REUNION FILLS US WITH HOPE FOR THE FUTURE

Encourage, console, strengthen, and cheer one another (v.18).

1) The grieving consoled. The believer in Jesus Christ, should not, as the unbelievers do, in the presence of death give way to hopeless grief.

2) Do you believe Jesus died and arose from the dead? Do you believe He is alive forevermore? Do you believe what He said: *"Because I live ye shall live also"*? Let this belief moderate your sorrow for the dead.

3) Do you expect the Lord's return? If so, you should not be troubled about the present condition and future state of departed saints. As the Lord's

death and resurrection are pledges of the resurrection and glorification of all who have died in the Lord, you should rejoice in the hope of an unending association with them in the city of God.

47. MAN'S LAST ENEMY CONQUERED

The last enemy that shall be destroyed is death. – 1
Corinthians 15:26

Christ—the greatness of his power—the certainty of his
triumph—the extent and duration of his reign, are the great
facts set forth here. Paul from his point of observation
sweeps the entire field of conflict, sees foe after foe falling
before the advancing conqueror until the last enemy has
surrendered and Christ is everywhere triumphant.

The text supplies us with a suitable and comforting theme
for this sad time and place in, *"Man's last enemy
conquered."*

1. DEATH IS AN ENEMY

Attempt to disguise it as you may by poetic description or
pleasing figures of speech, the fact remains that death is an
enemy. An enemy whom money cannot bribe—strength
defy, or power defeat. An enemy blind to our tears—deaf
to our prayers—unmindful of our grief. He has invaded
our homes and robbed them of their light and joy. He has
arrested our loved ones and borne them away to the
gloomy prison-house of the grave. He has compelled us
again and again in our anguish to cry out,

"Oh for the touch of a vanished hand,
And the sound of a voice that is still!"

What death has done for our friends he will surely do for
us. Each one of us can say with Job, *"For I know that those
will bring me to death and to the house appointed for all
living."* Some of us may die sooner than others, but all at
last. We are marching in a great procession toward the

grave. Death is an enemy, universal, untiring, irresistible, and cruel.

2. DEATH IS DESTROYED

1) The Scriptures declare it.

Marvel not at this: for the hour is coming, in the which all that are in the graves shall hear his voice, And shall come forth; they that have done good, unto the resurrection of life; and they that have done evil, unto the resurrection of damnation. – John 5:28-29

The chapter from which this text is taken is a masterly and unanswerable argument for the resurrection of the dead, and to every thoughtful person must put beyond reasonable question the fact of the final and irrecoverable overthrow of man's last enemy—Death.

2) Christ illustrated and proved the fact by raising from the dead the Ruler's daughter—the widow's son—Lazarus.

By his own resurrection, of which there can be no doubt. He then led captivity captive. His resurrection is the proof and pledge of ours. Our last enemy shall be destroyed!

Let this thought comfort us in this sad hour. We may be compelled to bury our loved ones, but they shall surely live again. We may see them, and know them, and live with them forever.

48. THE HEAVENLY MANSIONS

Let not your heart be troubled: ye believe in God, believe also in me. In my Father's house are many mansions: if it were not so, I would have told you. I go to prepare a place for you. And if I go and prepare a place for you, I will come again, and receive you unto myself; that where I am, there ye may be also. – John 14:1-3

1. THE MANSIONS DESCRIBED

"In my Father's House."

This description conveys the idea.

> 1) Of Locality. Where this house is, no one can say. But it must be where God is. Though He fills all places; though the heaven of heavens cannot contain Him, yet in the boundless universe there is one peculiar, appropriate, and magnificent place which He has allotted for Himself, His attendants and saints, to dwell in forever.
>
> That heaven is a *place* appears certain; because it is destined to receive into its spacious mansions at the last day, the glorified material bodies of all the saints; and even now that of Christ, and those of Enoch, Moses, and Elias, are there.
>
> Heaven has been too much considered as a *state* only, and not as a *place;* and thus it has lost much of the interest which it would have otherwise created in the mind. It is true that heaven derives its attractive influence from its being a *state* of happiness; for what is *place,* even the most beautiful, when the mind is unhappy?

2) Of Majesty. *"My Father's house."* The house of Deity. How magnificent must that house be which is the residence of the infinite Creator and Governor of all worlds—the Head of a boundless universe!

3) Of Home. *"My Father's house"* suggests this idea. From that house He came, and for a season dwelt in this world of sorrow. He therefore left His home, but having finished His work, was about to return.

2. THE MANSIONS EXPLORED

This representation of heaven implies,

1) Ample accommodation. *"Many mansions."*

2) Variety. *"Many mansions."* The sources of blessedness will be numerous and diverse.

3) Therefore the heavenly mansions will be infinitely suitable and adapted to sanctified souls. This is evident from what has already been stated:— the locality—the majesty, etc.

4) Mansions of stability. Not like a tent or tabernacle, always changing places.

5) Mansions of eternal permanency. "Mansions," in the original means to remain, to continue, or abiding places,—called in another place, "everlasting habitations."

49. WITH JESUS IN HEAVEN

1. THE LIGHT OF HEAVEN IS THE FACE OF JESUS

And they shall see his face; and his name shall be in their foreheads. And there shall be no night there; and they need no candle, neither light of the sun; for the Lord God giveth them light: and they shall reign for ever and ever. – Revelation 22:4-5

2. THE JOY OF HEAVEN IS THE PRESENCE OF JESUS

And I beheld, and, lo, in the midst of the throne and of the four beasts, and in the midst of the elders, stood a Lamb as it had been slain, having seven horns and seven eyes, which are the seven Spirits of God sent forth into all the earth. – Revelation 5:6

3. THE MELODY OF HEAVEN IS THE NAME OF JESUS

And I fell at his feet to worship him. And he said unto me, See thou do it not: I am thy fellowservant, and of thy brethren that have the testimony of Jesus: worship God: for the testimony of Jesus is the spirit of prophecy. – Revelation 19:10

4. THE HARMONY OF HEAVEN IS THE PRAISE OF JESUS

And every creature which is in heaven, and on the earth, and under the earth, and such as are in the sea, and all that are in them, heard I saying, Blessing, and honour, and glory, and power, be unto him that sitteth upon the throne, and unto the Lamb for ever and ever. – Revelation 5:13

5. THE THEME OFHEAVEN IS THE WORK OF JESUS

And when those beasts give glory and honour and thanks to him that sat on the throne, who liveth for ever and ever. – Revelation 4:9

6. THE FULLNESS OF HEAVEN IS JESUS HIMSELF

And I saw no temple therein: for the Lord God Almighty and the Lamb are the temple of it. – Revelation 21:22

50. THE BLESSING OF GOD'S SAINTS

1. SAINTS ARE CALLED TO AN ETERNAL GLORY

But the God of all grace, who hath called us unto his eternal glory by Christ Jesus, after that ye have suffered a while, make you perfect, stablish, strengthen, settle you. – 1 Peter 5:10

2. SAINTS ARE SAVED WITH AN ETERNAL SALVATION

And being made perfect, he became the author of eternal salvation unto all them that obey him. – Hebrews 5:9

3. SAINTS ARE BLESSED WITH AN ETERNAL PURPOSE

In whom also we have obtained an inheritance, being predestinated according to the purpose of him who worketh all things after the counsel of his own will. – Ephesians 1:11

4. SAINTS ARE PURCHASED WITH AN ETERNAL REDEMPTION

Neither by the blood of goats and calves, but by his own blood he entered in once into the holy place, having obtained eternal redemption for us. – Hebrews 9:12

5. SAINTS ARE SEALED WITH AN ETERNAL SPIRIT

How much more shall the blood of Christ, who through the eternal Spirit offered himself without spot to God, purge your conscience from dead works to serve the living God? – Hebrews 9:14

51. LIVING AND DYING AS A CHRISTIAN

For we know that if our earthly house of this tabernacle were dissolved, we have a building of God, an house not made with hands, eternal in the heavens. For in this we groan, earnestly desiring to be clothed upon with our house which is from heaven: If so be that being clothed we shall not be found naked. For we that are in this tabernacle do groan, being burdened: not for that we would be unclothed, but clothed upon, that mortality might be swallowed up of life. Now he that hath wrought us for the selfsame thing is God, who also hath given unto us the earnest of the Spirit. Therefore we are always confident, knowing that, whilst we are at home in the body, we are absent from the Lord: (For we walk by faith, not by sight:) We are confident, I say, and willing rather to be absent from the body, and to be present with the Lord. – 2 Corinthians 5:1-8

1. WE HAVE A BUILDING FROM GOD

Let not your heart be troubled: ye believe in God, believe also in me. In my Father's house are many mansions: if it were not so, I would have told you. I go to prepare a place for you. And if I go and prepare a place for you, I will come again, and receive you unto myself; that where I am, there ye may be also. – John 14:1-3

Blessed be the God and Father of our Lord Jesus Christ, which according to his abundant mercy hath begotten us again unto a lively hope by the resurrection of Jesus Christ from the dead, To an inheritance incorruptible, and undefiled, and that fadeth not away, reserved in heaven for you, Who are kept by the power of God through faith unto salvation ready to be revealed in the last time. – 1 Peter 1:3-5

Therefore, my beloved brethren, be ye stedfast, unmoveable, always abounding in the work of the Lord, forasmuch as ye know that your labour is not in vain in the Lord. – 1 Corinthians 15:58

TO LIVE AS A CHRISTIAN IS TO LIVE A LIFE OF HOPE.

2. WE GROAN AS WE LONG FOR THAT DAY

In Christ we have a deep longing for our reward.

1) To have that home, John 14:1-3 (above).

2) To be with Jesus.

Beloved, now are we the sons of God, and it doth not yet appear what we shall be: but we know that, when he shall appear, we shall be like him; for we shall see him as he is. – 1 John 3:2

3) To leave behind pain and sorrow of this world.

And I heard a great voice out of heaven saying, Behold, the tabernacle of God is with men, and he will dwell with them, and they shall be his people, and God himself shall be with them, and be their God. And God shall wipe away all tears from their eyes; and there shall be no more death, neither sorrow, nor crying, neither shall there be any more pain: for the former things are passed away. And he that sat upon the throne said, Behold, I make all things new. And he said unto me, Write: for these words are true and faithful. And he said unto me, It is done. I am Alpha and Omega, the beginning and the end. I will give unto him that is athirst of the fountain of the water of life freely. He that overcometh shall inherit all things; and I will be his God, and he shall be my son. – Revelation 21:3-7

TO LIVE AS A CHRISTIAN IS TO LIVE A LIFE OF GROANING.

3. WE LIVE AND DIE CONFIDENTLY

1) Like Peter

And Simon Peter answered and said, Thou art the Christ, the Son of the living God. – Matthew 16:16

Because it is written, Be ye holy; for I am holy. And if ye call on the Father, who without respect of persons judgeth according to every man's work, pass the time of your sojourning *here* in fear. – 1 Peter 1:16-17

2) Like Paul

For the which cause I also suffer these things: nevertheless I am not ashamed: for I know whom I have believed, and am persuaded that he is able to keep that which I have committed unto him against that day. – 2 Timothy 1:12

3) Like John

And many other signs truly did Jesus in the presence of his disciples, which are not written in this book: But these are written, that ye might believe that Jesus is the Christ, the Son of God; and that believing ye might have life through his name. – John 20:30-31

That which we have seen and heard declare we unto you, that ye also may have fellowship with us: and truly our fellowship is with the Father, and with his Son Jesus Christ. – 1 John 1:3

TO LIVE AS A CHRISTIAN IS TO LIVE A LIFE OF CONFIDENCE.

52. THE FAITH AND HOPE
OF JOB IN HIS REDEEMER

For I know that my redeemer liveth, and that he shall stand at the latter day upon the earth: And though after my skin worms destroy this body, yet in my flesh shall I see God: Whom I shall see for myself, and mine eyes shall behold, and not another; though my reins be consumed within me. – Job 19:25-27

Job was weighed down by a heavy load of afflictions, and misrepresented by his mistaken friends, yet he looked forward to the coming of his Redeemer; and had a comfortable assurance that he would avenge his wrongs, raise him from the dead, and bless him with the heavenly vision.

1. JOB HAD A LIVING REDEEMER

1) Christ is the Redeemer of men. He bought us with His blood. We *"were not redeemed with corruptible things, as silver and gold, but with the precious blood of Christ, as a Lamb without blemish and without spot"* (1 Pet. 1:19). He saves and delivers His people from the guilt and power, and from the pollution and punishment of sin. He *"gave Himself for us, that He might redeem us from all iniquity, and purify unto Himself a peculiar people, zealous of good works"* (Tit. 2:14). And He will vindicate and avenge His church: in allusion to this, He says, *"The day of vengeance is in My heart, and the year of My redeemer is come"* (Isa. 63:4).

2) The Son of God, our Great Redeemer, was living in the days of Job; and he had a saving interest in him, in the afflictions which he suffered from the

devil and from men. He says, *"My Redeemer liveth."* If our Lord had no existence prior to His incarnation, Job should have spoken in the future tense, saying, "I know that my Redeemer shall live;" but he spoke correctly, for his Redeemer was then living. He had glory with the Father *"before the world was"* (John 17:5). He was rich in a prior state of existence, yet for our sakes *"He became poor"* (2 Cor. 8:9). He was the only begotten Son of the Father (John 3:16).

3) Job knew his Divine Redeemer. But how did he attain that knowledge? It might be by tradition. God had promised a Savior and deliverer, and that promise was handed down from one generation to another. Besides, the promise which was given to Abraham, *"In thy seed shall all the nations of the earth be blessed,"* was probably well known to Job; but it is most probable he knew his Redeemer by immediate revelation. God might make a discovery of this great truth to him,—first, to support him on his unparalleled affliction; and, secondly, to comfort and encourage the Church in the ages to come.

2. JOB HAD A JOYFUL HOPE OF RESURRECTION FROM THE DEAD

1) He positively affirms that, after the destruction of his body, he should see God in his flesh. But how can that be the case, either with him or others, if the dead do not rise? Man was created with a body, and will live in an embodied state, to all eternity; but that cannot be without a resurrection, because his earthly and material frame returns to dust, as a sad punishment of his apostasy from God (Gen. 3:19).

How God will raise the dead is unknown; but the fact is certain. It was revealed to Job, and has been undeniably proved by the resurrection of Jesus. With these eyes of flesh we shall see God our Savior. What a happy sight! Then the sorrows of life will be past, death will be destroyed, and a blessed eternity will follow!

2) I shall see for myself, he says, *"and mine eyes shall behold, and not another."* Good men wish well to all; but they claim the blessings of grace and glory as their own. Others, no doubt, will see and enjoy the Redeemer; but I shall see and enjoy Him for myself. He will appear in my cause; He will deliver me from death and the grave; He will vindicate my character; and He will avenge me of my foes. And all this will take place, though my body fails completely; for all things are possible with God; and He who made the world can raise the dead.

THANK YOU FOR
INVESTING IN THIS BOOK!

We'd love to hear your feedback. Please stop by and leave a review at: **http://www.amazon.com/author/barrydavis**. You can also check out our other books there.

If you'd like to see some of our many resources for Bible Study leaders and Pastors, please go to:
http://www.pastorshelper.com

I hope to hear from you soon! May God bless you as you continue to serve Him.

In Christ,

Barry L. Davis

Made in the USA
Monee, IL
21 July 2022

10083840R00075